PAUL BOCUSE
France

Avec toute ma
sympathie gourmande

Paul Bocuse

1999

Paul Bocuse
France

Paul Bocuse's Regional French Cooking

With the Assistance of
Martine Albertin, Anne Grandclément, and Pascale Couderc
Translated by Stephanie Curtis
Recipes adapted from the French by Stephanie Curtis
and Charles Pierce
Photography by Dietmar Frege

Flammarion
Paris - New York

Edited by Julie Gaskill
Designed by Marc Walter
Typesetting by Optigraphic, Paris
and Octavo Editions, Paris
Color separation by Colourscan France
Printed and bound by Canale, Turin

Flammarion
26, rue Racine
75006 Paris

200 Park Avenue South
Suite 1406
New York, NY 10003

Original title: *Cuisine de France*
Copyright © 1991 Flammarion

CIP data may be found on page 192.

For the English translation:
Copyright © 1991 Flammarion.

First paperback edition:
Copyright © 1997 Flammarion.

ISBN: 2-08013-641-0
Numéro d'édition: 1260
Dépôt légal: February 1997

Printed in Italy by G. Canale & C. - Turin

CONTENTS

T his is not my first cookbook, as some of you may have noticed. And you might ask yourselves what could be so new and remarkable in French cooking that I insist upon writing about it once again.

What is remarkable today is that despite new trends and a cooking revolution, tradition has never been stronger. Of course, to say that all the fads and innovations that have passed through French kitchens in recent years have contributed nothing would be untrue. In the 1990s we no longer eat as we did at the turn of the century: we consume less, we try to balance dietary fats, and we watch our sugar intake. We take care of ourselves, emphasizing moderation while realizing that delight in good food is also an indispensable ingredient at our tables.

"One of the pleasures of living in the country is watching vegetables grow in one's own garden. It makes me feel very fortunate."

We therefore place more importance on the best products, food that has genuine flavor: beautifully ripened cheeses, creamy butter, fish that shines with freshness, free-range chickens fed on grain, farm-raised beef, aromatic fruits and vegetables, and fresh, wholesome breads. In short, we have finally understood that we can not produce healthy, flavorful cooking, nor even dietetic fare, without beginning with quality materials. After a period of producing bland, over-sterilized products, the food industry decided to apply its *savoir-faire* and technical expertise to the quest for real taste. And even if fast-food shops continue to sprout in France and elsewhere like so many mushrooms, home-style dishes, lovingly simmered in the old-fashioned way with patience and care, are not losing ground—in fact, they are coming back into favor. In this book, I would like to prove this to you, and remind you that the best soups are often made in the oldest pots.

I would like this book to be leafed through, read at

leisure, and used like a stroll around France. A stroll through time, occasionally, when a recipe is traced to another century or a particular historic event. A stroll by a traveler who is following his taste buds and curiosity from region to region, and who finds the essence of that region in the steam that wafts from its saucepans. There is more to France than its museums and the cool stone of its old cathedrals. France must be breathed, tasted, and absorbed.

Some readers may not agree with the way I have geographically "annexed" what may be their favorite region. I can already hear the complaints about my expansionist tendencies, at least those that lead me to place under Lyonnais dominion a collection of territories and culinary traditions which, though neighboring, are not without their own originality. I could blame it on the editors and their penchant to divide everything into neat, precise little categories. But that would be a lie; it took no less than three of them to keep me from carrying the Lyonnais connection too far. Sometimes I regret having given in; there was something intoxicating about the game. Nevertheless, I have tried, wherever possible, to provide the identity and background of each recipe, respecting the character of local products and regional methods. I have, in some cases, lightened or adapted; that is one of the advantages of tradition — it is more flexible than we think, and many variations can be drawn from it. In some cases, I have stayed with the most classic interpretation. I hope that *Regional French Cooking*, the authentic *cuisine française*, that which rises above current fad and fashion but that is also flexible enough to adapt to the times, will become your own, along with the pleasure of rediscovered flavors.

"There is harmony in the colors and forms of a beautiful cheese tray: white "barattes" bring out the rosy grey of the Charolais; the sturdy, solid Tome de Savoie with the Reblochon, soft to the touch; the Saint Marcellin, at the height of its maturity..."

"The vegetable garden is right next to the restaurant. It is the domain of Marcel Besson, or "Bobosse," as we call him, who for the past eight years has kept me informed on the arrival of the first green beans, the well-being of the cardoons, and the demise of the last snow peas."

LYONNAIS

W hat is the Lyonnais? This is a difficult question to answer. The Lyonnais is here, it is my region, but it is also elsewhere. The more I look at the map of France, the more I feel that when the French gather around the table, they are all cousins. Still, I have to admit that this region is privileged, and that it has a reputation for delicious food; one that is borne out by the *gourmandise* of the local populace. Lyon, true to its image, is a city that whets the appetite. Not a morning goes by at Lyon's Part-Dieu market that I do not meet my old friends to share a Lyonnais snack, or *mâchon*, as we call it:

a dozen oysters, a *sabaudet* sausage, a steaming bowl of the local tripe stew (*tablier de sapeur*), and a mutton-foot salad.

The tradition of the *mâchon* dates back to Lyon's silk workers, the *canuts*, who alleviated the drudgery of their arduous occupation by escaping for a few moments of liberty and gustatory pleasure. In Lyon, the *mâchon* is the market worker's breakfast, a complete meal washed down with Beaujolais: not recommended for small appetites. It is a rite of passage, essential for anyone

claiming to be *de Lyon*, even if only for one day, and a prerequisite for feeling at home throughout the region.

For me, the Lyonnais encompasses Burgundy, with its vineyards and its own exceptional culinary tradition that makes it yet another center of French gastronomy. It includes Dijon, with its mustard, *cassis, pain d'épices*, its *jambon persillé* and crayfish; the Bresse region, famous for its chickens and capons; the Charolais, with its prize-winning beef; and an area famous for its freshwater fish, the Dombes. The Franc-Comtois, who speak with an accent similar to our own, also belong to the larger family of the Lyonnais, and bring us their Bleu de Septmoncel, Morbier and Comté cheeses, and their nutty *vins jaunes*. Finally, the Lyonnais includes the valley of the Saône river, rich with fruits and vegetables, and parts of nearby Savoie and Auvergne. It is a surprisingly vast area and, not surprisingly perhaps, a region well supplied with fabulous cooks and excellent chefs.

Cabbage Soup

(Soupe au chou)

Since the Middle Ages we have known the virtues—both medicinal and culinary—of cabbage, which is the king vegetable of all self-respecting peasant soups. In the Auvergne, where "a chou *is still a* chou," *as an old saying goes, it is claimed that the best soups are made from cabbages that have been through a frost.*

Cut the bacon into 1 by 1 1/2-inch pieces. Fill a large saucepan with 3 quarts water.

Add the bacon.

Bring to a boil and let simmer for 10 minutes, skimming off the foam that rises to the top.

Peel off and discard the outer leaves of the cabbage. Rinse and quarter the head. Place in a large saucepan of boiling water and blanch for 5 minutes. Remove and drain.

Peel the carrots and turnips. Trim and thoroughly rinse the leeks. Cut the carrots, turnips, and leeks into large pieces. Peel and quarter the potatoes. Add the carrots, turnips and leeks to the saucepan with the bacon. Peel the onion and stick it with the clove. Add to the saucepan along with the suet.

Bring to a boil. Add a generous sprinkling of coarse salt and a few white peppercorns. Cover and let simmer gently for 25 minutes.

Add the potatoes and let simmer, covered, 20 minutes longer or until the potatoes are tender.

To serve, place a slice of crusty country-style bread in the bottom of 6 shallow soup plates. Ladle the soup over the top and serve.

FOR 6 SERVINGS

3/4 pound slab bacon
3 quarts water
1 large head savoy cabbage
3 carrots
2 turnips
2 leeks
5 firm medium potatoes
1 large onion
1 clove
1 tablespoon suet or bacon fat
Coarse salt
White peppercorns
6 thick slices country-style bread

Cooking time:
1 hour 5 minutes

Pumpkin Soup

(Soupe au potiron)

In the Lyonnais, we call this gourd soup. We also make gratins and purées with pumpkin, and, in the North, it is baked into pies. Unfortunately, pumpkin is a vegetable that is too often overlooked in those regions where it is not part of a culinary tradition.

Available in the market from fall to December, it can be stored, whole, for long periods.

Slice off the top of the pumpkin as evenly as possible, and scoop out and discard the seeds and stringy fiber. Delicately scoop out the pumpkin flesh, being careful not to puncture the outer shell. (The scooped-out shell will be used as a tureen for serving the pumpkin soup.)

Cut the pumpkin flesh into cubes. Place in a steamer basket over simmering water and steam for about 20 minutes, or until fork-tender.

Place the chicken stock in a small saucepan and warm over medium heat. Transfer the steamed pumpkin to the bowl of a food processor and process to a purée, adding the hot stock little by little.

Turn the mixture into a medium saucepan, stir in the crème fraîche and mix thoroughly.

Season to taste with the salt, pepper and grated nutmeg.

Bring to a boil over medium heat. Let boil gently for a few minutes.

Pour the hot soup into the scooped-out pumpkin shell. Chop the chervil. Sprinkle with the croutons and the chervil, and serve.

FOR 6 SERVINGS

1 small pumpkin
(about 4 1/2 pounds)
1/2 cup chicken bouillon
1 cup crème fraîche
or heavy cream
Salt
Freshly ground pepper
Freshly ground nutmeg
Fresh chervil sprigs
Toasted croutons

Cooking time:
About 30 minutes

2 1/4 pounds leeks
1 pound white potatoes
5 tablespoons unsalted
butter
2 quarts water
1 sprig fresh thyme
1 sprig parsley
Salt
Freshly ground pepper
1 1/4 cups heavy cream
1 tablespoon chives,
chopped

Cooking time:
50 minutes

Leek and Potato Soup

(Vichyssoise)

A chef from the Bourbonnais region created this cold leek and potato soup at New York's Ritz Carlton around the turn of the century.

His vichyssoise *was an instant success, and served, both in the New World and in France, as an example of* la grande cuisine française.

It is only natural, therefore, that we list it in our inventory of national recipes. There is also a vichyssoise à la Ritz *that includes a little tomato, but the authentic soup is still made of potatoes, leeks and cream, and nothing else.*

Peel the leeks, trimming off and discarding the dark green part. Cut a deep slit down the side of each and rinse thoroughly under cold water to remove all sand. Drain and chop coarsely.

Rinse, peel and dice the potatoes.

Melt the butter in a large saucepan. Add the leeks and cook over low heat until soft but not browned. Stir in the potatoes.

Add the water, thyme, and parsley, and season with salt and pepper.

Bring to a boil and let simmer gently for about 35 minutes.

Drain the leeks and potatoes, reserving a little of the cooking liquid. Place the drained vegetables in a food processor or a blender and process to a purée.

Transfer the purée to a clean saucepan with about 1 cup of the cooking liquid and the cream. Bring to a boil over medium heat, whisking constantly.

Remove from the heat and let cool to room temperature before placing in the refrigerator to chill for 2 hours.

Just before serving, correct the seasoning and chop the chives.

Ladle the *vichyssoise* into consommé bowls and sprinkle with the chives.

Lyon-style Onion Soup

(Gratinée lyonnaise)

*I*n Lyon we put onions in almost everything, and we even claim the copyright on the celebrated onion soup that the Ile-de-France and specifically Les Halles market in Paris adopted as their own, with a few modifications. Let them keep their version. Here is the real Lyonnais gratinée, the way we like it chez nous.

Peel the onions and slice as thinly as possible.

Melt 4 tablespoons of the butter in a Dutch oven or other large heavy pot. Add the onions and sauté, stirring frequently.

When the onions are nicely browned, sprinkle them evenly with the flour. Let cook for a minute longer, then add the water or bouillon. Season to taste with the salt and pepper. (If using bouillon or stock, be careful not to add too much salt.)

Cook at a gentle boil for 30 minutes. Meanwhile, slice the bread thinly and toast lightly. Grate half of the cheese and cut the other half into thin slices.

In the bottom of an ovenproof soup tureen place the remaining tablespoon of butter and a little of the grated cheese. Add a layer of toasted bread slices. Cover with thin slices of cheese.

Continue to layer the grated cheese, toast, and sliced cheese, alternating layers. Thoroughly wet the ingredients with a small amount of the broth. Place under a hot broiler to grill until all of the liquid is completely absorbed.

Add the remaining broth and the cognac. Place in the oven for 10 minutes longer.

In a small bowl, combine the egg yolk and the port, if using, and whisk until well blended. Just before serving the soup, pour this mixture over the top of the tureen.

This soup should be served very hot, nearly boiling.

FOR 4 SERVINGS

3/4 pound yellow onions
5 tablespoons unsalted butter
1/4 cup flour
Salt
Freshly ground pepper
6 cups water or beef bouillon
1/2 loaf French-style crusty bread
or 4 slices firm white bread
3/4 pound Gruyère cheese or other Swiss-style cheese
1/3 cup cognac
1 egg yolk (optional)
3/4 cup port wine (optional)

*Cooking time:
1 hour*

Herbed Fresh Cheese

(Cervelle de canut)

The French name means "silk workers' brains," a barbaric sobriquet perhaps, but this Lyonnais favorite is nothing more than creamy fresh cheese, beaten well and seasoned with herbs, shallots, salt, pepper and white wine vinegar. Serve it in shallow bowls as a starter, or as the cheese course after the meal with slices of toasted country-style bread.

Snip the leaves from the chervil, tarragon and parsley, discarding the stems, and chop each variety separately. Peel the shallots and chop them finely.

Combine the *fromage blanc* and vinegar in a mixing bowl and beat well. Add the olive oil and beat well. Stir in the chopped chervil, tarragon, parsley, chives, and shallots. Squeeze the garlic through a garlic press and add to the mixture. Season with salt and pepper. Beat well and chill for 2 hours.

Note: *Fromage blanc* is a snow-white, fresh, creamy cheese usually made from cow's milk. French brands are exported to the United States and can be found in specialty food shops. If it is not available, its taste and texture can be simulated by beating 1/2 pint heavy cream with 2 8-ounce packages of whipped cream cheese in a mixing bowl or food processor.

FOR 6 SERVINGS

10 sprigs fresh chervil
6 sprigs fresh tarragon
8 sprigs flat parsley
1 tablespoon chives, chopped
4 shallots
2 1/2 cups fresh *fromage blanc* (see note)
2 tablespoons white wine vinegar
2 tablespoons olive oil
1 clove garlic
Salt
Pepper

Preparation time: 15 minutes

Baked Eggs and Onions

(Œufs "à la tripe")

A simple combination of hard-cooked eggs in a béchamel sauce with onions, the origin of the name of this typically Lyonnais dish remains a mystery. For some, the thinly sliced onions bring to mind gras-double or Lyonnais-style honeycomb tripe, and thus the appellation à la tripe.

Others claim that the dish was a favorite snack of Lyon's tripe-sellers.

Peel the onions, cut them in half, and slice them finely. Plunge them into a saucepan of boiling water, blanch for 5 minutes and drain.

Place the onions in a large saucepan and cook over low heat to dry up excess water.

Add the butter, let it melt over the onions and cook, stirring with a wooden spoon until the onions are lightly browned.

Sprinkle the flour evenly over the onions and stir to mix.

Add the chicken stock to the onions a little at a time, stirring constantly. Season with the nutmeg, salt and pepper.

Let simmer over low heat, stirring constantly, for 20 minutes.

Place the eggs in a large saucepan of boiling water and cook for 10 minutes. Drain and rinse eggs under cold water, peel and slice into 1/4-inch rounds.

Ladle half of the sauce into an ovenproof *gratin* dish. Arrange the hard-boiled egg slices evenly over the sauce, and spoon the remaining sauce over the top.

FOR 6 SERVINGS

1 pound onions
(about 5 medium)
1/2 cup unsalted butter
5 tablespoons flour
3 1/4 cups chicken
bouillon (or milk)
Pinch ground nutmeg
Salt
Pepper
9 eggs

Cooking time:
35 minutes

24

Cheese Soufflé

(Soufflé au fromage)

This is undoubtedly the most classic of soufflés, and one of the least pretentious. Proust's Françoise would have said that it takes a certain knack to make it. My hint is simply to use more egg yolks than whites. I have used Gruyère in this soufflé, but other Swiss-style or hard cheeses like Comté also produce excellent results.

Melt 2 tablespoons of the butter in a medium saucepan over low heat. Add the flour and stir with a wooden spoon until the mixture begins to foam, then let cook for about a minute longer without allowing it to brown.

Stir in the milk and water and let cook for 5 to 6 minutes, stirring constantly. Remove from the heat and season with salt. Cool slightly.

Preheat the oven to 375° F.

Separate the eggs, placing the 3 egg whites in a very clean mixing bowl. (Any speck of dirt or grease on the bowl will prevent the whites from reaching their full volume. To insure a perfectly clean surface, run a lemon wedge over the sides and bottom of the bowl, then dry with a clean towel.) Using an electric beater, beat the whites until very firm.

In a separate bowl, beat the 4 yolks lightly. Stir the yolks into the cooled béchamel sauce. Add the grated cheese. Season with salt, pepper and a pinch of nutmeg. Using a rubber spatula, gently fold the whites into the mixture, being careful not to deflate them.

Butter a 6-cup soufflé mold or charlotte mold with the remaining butter. Turn the soufflé mixture into the mold, filling it to about 3/4 full.

Place on the center rack of the preheated oven and bake for 20 minutes. Remove from the oven and serve immediately.

FOR 4 SERVINGS

3 tablespoons unsalted butter
2 tablespoons flour
1/2 cup milk
1/2 cup water
Salt
3 eggs
1 egg yolk
1 1/2 cups grated Gruyère cheese
Pepper
Grated nutmeg

Special equipment:
6-cup soufflé mold

Cooking time:
About 25 minutes

1 Lyon-style pork and pistachio sausage (see note)
2 1/4 pounds new or red-skin potatoes
1 tablespoon coarse salt
6 tablespoons dry white wine, preferably Mâcon
2 tablespoons Dijon mustard
1 tablespoon white wine vinegar
Salt
Freshly ground pepper
3 tablespoons vegetable oil
2 shallots
2 sprigs flat-leaf parsley
5 sprigs fresh chervil

Cooking time for the sausage: 30 minutes

Potato and Pistachio Sausage Salad

(Salade de pommes de terre et saucisson pistaché)

The variety of la charcuterie lyonnaise *is inexhaustible, and this naturally applies to sausages, both dried and fresh. One of my favorites is* saucisson pistaché, *a fresh savory pork sausage studded with pistachios. It can be served as it is here, sliced in a salad of potatoes cooked in their skins, or simply* à la lyonnaise, *meaning with steamed potatoes, or à* l'anglaise, *with a mound of fresh butter to make the combination even more mouthwatering.*

Place the sausage (without pricking the skin) in a large saucepan, adding enough cold water to cover generously. Bring to a simmer and let cook at a very gentle simmer without boiling for 30 minutes. Remove the saucepan from the heat and let the sausage poach in the hot water for 5 more minutes.

Place the unpeeled potatoes in a saucepan of cold water with the coarse salt and cook for about 20 minutes, or until tender.

Drain and peel the potatoes. Slice into rounds and place in a mixing bowl. Sprinkle with the white wine while they are still warm.

Prepare the vinaigrette: combine the mustard, vinegar, salt, pepper and oil in a small bowl. Pour the vinaigrette over the potatoes and toss gently.

Peel and chop the shallots. Remove the leaves from the parsley and chervil and chop them finely.

Slice the sausage into thick rounds. Arrange the potatoes and warm sausage on a serving platter. Sprinkle with the shallots, parsley and chervil, and serve.

Note: If pistachio sausage is not available, substitute a good-quality fresh, unsmoked, firmly packed pork sausage. Fresh, unsmoked garlic sausages can be bought in some ethnic markets. Polish sausages such as kielbasa can also be substituted.

Savoie-style Potatoes and Cheese
(Tartiflette)

*T*he name is a local term used in the Haute-Savoie to describe a preparation of potatoes (called *tartoufle* in the eighteenth century) crowned with a split round of soft, mountain Reblochon cheese and baked in the oven. The tartiflette *from the Annecy region is a meal in itself, and if you ever indulge in one there, you can be sure that you will not go away hungry.*

Rinse the potatoes, place them in a large saucepan, cover generously with cold water, and add the coarse salt. Bring to a simmer and let cook for 20 minutes until fork-tender but still slightly "al dente." Drain, peel and cut the potatoes into thick rounds.

Slice the smoked bacon or ham into 1 by 1/4-inch pieces. Plunge them into a pan of boiling water and blanch for 1 minute. Drain and pat dry. Peel the onions, and slice them thinly.

Preheat the oven to 350° F.

Melt the butter in a saucepan, add the bacon and onions, and cook over medium heat until lightly browned. Add the potatoes and let simmer for 15 minutes. Stir in the white wine.

Turn the mixture into a buttered *gratin* dish large enough to easily contain all ingredients.

Cut the Reblochon disk in half horizontally and arrange the two halves, crust sides down, over the potatoes.

Cover with aluminum foil and cook in the preheated oven for 30 minutes.

Serve as a main course with a green salad.

Note: Apremont is a dry white wine from the Savoie region.

Reblochon is a disk-shaped, creamy cow's milk cheese with a mild, nutty flavor. If you can not find it, several wedges (about one pound) of a very ripe Brie, cut in half horizontally, can be substituted.

FOR 6 SERVINGS

1 pound potatoes
Coarse salt
3/4 pound slab bacon or 1 thick slice smoked ham
2 medium onions
1 tablespoon unsalted butter
3/4 cup Apremont or other dry white wine (see note)
1 ripened round Reblochon cheese, approximately one pound (see note)
Salt
Pepper

Cooking time:
1 hour 10 minutes

1 free-range capon
(7 to 8 pounds),
with liver and gizzards
Salt
Freshly ground pepper
1 large black truffle
1 tablespoon olive oil
4 1/2 pounds chestnuts
3 1/2 tablespoons unsalted
butter
6 cups chicken bouillon
2 ribs celery with leaves
5 sprigs chervil

*Cooking time for capon:
2 hours 35 minutes*

Roast Capon with Chestnuts

(Chapon rôti aux marrons)

This dish is served at Christmas, when the Bresse capons first appear in the markets. Chestnuts, too, are plentiful during this season.

A capon is a young rooster that has been castrated and raised as a coq en pâte, *or in a coop. Nothing is allowed to disturb these coddled cocks—their vocation is to eat. In my opinion the best capons are from Bresse, and have the same appellation as the* poulardes fines *(fine hens) described by the eighteenth-century author and gastronome Brillat-Savarin. Their dense and melting meat is unlike any other; and the best way to cook them is still on the spit over an open fire. If that is not possible, cook them in the oven.*

Preheat the oven to 325° F.

Remove the liver and gizzards from the capon, rinse the cavity and pat dry. Season the cavity with salt and pepper.

Tuck the liver, gizzards and truffle back into the cavity and truss the capon.

31

Rub the oil over the skin of the bird and season generously with salt and pepper.

Place the capon in a baking pan and cook in the preheated oven for 2 1/2 hours, basting the bird with its juices several times during the cooking.

Meanwhile, prepare the chestnuts: slit the rounded side of the shell of each chestnut. Place in a large saucepan of boiling salted water and cook for a few minutes. Drain and peel the chestnuts while still warm, removing both the shell and the underlying white skin.

Melt the butter in a large skillet. Add the chestnuts and stir with a wooden spoon to coat with a film of butter. Add the celery ribs. Pour the bouillon over all. Cover and let simmer, without stirring, for about 20 minutes.

Drain the chestnuts, discarding the celery, and add them to the pan with the capon 5 minutes before the bird has finished cooking.

Remove the capon from the oven. Arrange the chestnuts on a vegetable dish and sprinkle with the chopped chervil.

Remove the truffle, liver and gizzards from the bird's cavity. Cut the truffle into thin slices and dice the liver and gizzards. Sprinkle these over the chestnuts.

Carve the capon and arrange it on a large warm serving platter.

Deglaze the baking pan with about 1/4 cup water or stock, stirring with a wooden spoon to detach the browned bits that stick to the bottom, and let simmer briefly. Pour into a sauceboat.

Note: Frozen or vacuum-packed chestnuts may also be used.

"Traditionally, the French eat capon at Christmas, but the recipe I have given here will also work well with a Bresse or other free-range chicken."

Cock in Red Wine
(Coq au vin)

FOR 8 SERVINGS

1 Bresse or free-range cock, about 6 1/2 pounds
2 quarts red Burgundy wine
1 onion
2 carrots
2 sprigs fresh thyme
1/2 bay leaf
Peppercorns
3 tablespoons vegetable oil
3 cloves garlic
1 teaspoon salt
1/2 pound slab bacon
1/2 pound cultivated white mushrooms
1/4 pound pearl onions
2 tablespoons unsalted butter
10 sprigs parsley

Cooking time for the cock: From 1 to 2 hours depending on its age

I n the Burgundy of the past, roosters weighed six to seven pounds at least, and worked hard all their lives running after hens before ending up in the stock pot. They were tough old birds and needed to be braised slowly in generous amounts of liquid to prevent them from drying out. The roosters that we find in the market today labeled coq au vin, *meaning to be cooked with wine, are less muscular and require a shorter cooking time. But the wine used in the preparation is, of course, always a Burgundy, whether a simple Passetoutgrain or a nobler Chambertin.*

Begin preparing the bird a day in advance. Rinse it, pat dry and cut into 10 pieces. Place in a mixing bowl with the wine.

Peel and thinly slice the onion. Peel the carrots and cut into thin rounds. Add the onion, carrots, thyme, bay leaf and peppercorns to the chicken and wine. Cover and refrigerate overnight.

The following day, remove the chicken and vegetables from the marinade, drain and pat dry. Strain the marinade through a fine sieve and reserve.

Heat the oil in a large, deep-sided skillet. Add the chicken, a few pieces at a time, sauté until nicely browned on all sides, and transfer to a large Dutch oven. Sauté the vegetables in the skillet until lightly browned and add to the Dutch oven. Crush the garlic and add to the skillet. Pour the marinade into the Dutch oven and season with salt.

Bring to a boil over medium heat, then cover and simmer over low heat for 1 to 2 hours, depending on the age of the bird.

Remove any rind from the slab bacon and cut into 1 by 1/4-inch pieces. Rinse and trim the mushrooms. Peel the pearl onions. Melt the butter in a skillet, add the bacon, mushrooms, and onions, and sauté until browned, about 8 minutes.

A few minutes before the chicken is ready to serve, add the sautéed bacon, mushrooms and onions to the pan and cook, stirring, until heated through. Correct the seasoning. Mince the parsley, sprinkle over the chicken and serve.

Note: The flavor and authenticity of this dish depend on finding, as we have noted above, a "tough old bird." If you can not get a rooster, buy the biggest, oldest hen you can find. You may have to buy two smaller chickens. The younger the chicken, the shorter the cooking time.

Hen with Crayfish

(Poularde aux écrevisses)

Talking about traditional and regional recipes can bring on a certain nostalgia. For example: the crayfish trawling of my childhood. Is it the grande cuisine of the past three centuries that has nearly exhausted this species by including them in every sauce, bisque, and boudin? Or is it the deterioration of our rivers and streams and widespread poaching that have made them so scarce? It takes at least five years for a crayfish to reach maturity. Longer, at any rate, than for the hen that accompanies them in the traditional Burgundian recipe that follows.

Note: The species called for here, red-clawed crayfish, is the best. But when I can not find these, I use a small lobster, cooked, shelled, and cut into rounds. The lobster coral can be used to bind the sauce, and poulet aux écrevisses becomes poulet au homard.

Peel and chop the shallots. Peel, seed, and chop the tomatoes.

Heat the oil in a large, deep-sided skillet or heavy saucepan.

Add the shallots and cook until transparent. Remove them from the pan and reserve.

Cut up the chicken and add to the pan, a few pieces at a time, letting it brown on all sides. Season with salt and pepper.

Remove the chicken and keep it warm.

Add the crayfish to the pan and cook over high heat, stirring with a wooden spoon. Cover and cook for 5 minutes.

Remove the crayfish and keep warm. Return the chicken and shallots to the pan, add the white wine, and bring to a boil. Add the tomatoes, cook and reduce briefly. Add the hot bouillon and continue to cook over medium heat for about 25 minutes. Transfer the chicken to a heated platter and keep warm.

Separate the heads from the crayfish tails, emptying the liquid contents of the heads into the saucepan and placing it over medium heat for 3 minutes. Remove the crayfish tails from their shells and add the meat to the platter with the chicken. Strain the sauce through a fine sieve, and return it to the saucepan. Cut the butter into small pieces and whisk it into the sauce a few pieces at a time, moving the saucepan on and off the heat until the sauce is thick and smooth.

Pour the sauce over all and serve immediately.

FOR 6 SERVINGS

2 shallots
2 tomatoes
2 tablespoons oil
1 Bresse or free-range hen (about 5 pounds)
Salt
Pepper
24 red-clawed crayfish
3/4 cup dry white wine, preferably Mâcon
3/4 cup hot chicken bouillon
4 tablespoons unsalted butter

Cooking time:
1 hour

36

Bresse Chicken in Vinegar

(Poulet de Bresse au vinaigre)

It is a chicken from Bresse, naturally, that stars in this recipe. That alone is enough to make this a dish typical of the area. Then there is the vinegar, which the Lyonnais love to add as a finishing touch to so many of their delectable creations. This chicken in vinegar is probably a descendant of a recipe of the Middle Ages that called for verjus, *the tart juice of unripened grapes. The success of this dish depends greatly on the type of vinegar used. In this region of vineyards and good wines it would be unforgivable to use anything but the best.*

Rinse the chicken and cut it into 8 pieces. Peel, seed and chop the tomatoes.

In a large Dutch oven, melt 2 tablespoons of the butter with the oil. Add the chicken pieces and cook, turning, until browned on all sides. Season with salt and pepper. Add the garlic cloves (unpeeled) and mix well.

Add the vinegar and bring to a boil. Stir in the tomatoes, cover the pan and let cook over medium heat for 25 minutes.

Transfer the chicken pieces to a warmed ovenproof platter and keep warm while preparing the sauce.

Add the bouillon to the pan and cook, stirring and scraping the pan with a wooden spoon to detach the flavorful browned bits that stick to the bottom. Reduce over high heat by about one-third.

Strain the sauce through a sieve, pressing the garlic cloves with the back of a spoon to extract their flavor. Cut the remaining butter into small pieces and add to the sauce, a piece or two at a time, whisking over low heat after each addition. Stir in the cream.

Pour the sauce over the chicken pieces, decorate with the chervil and serve.

FOR 4 SERVINGS

1 large Bresse or free-range chicken (about 3 1/2 pounds)
2 tomatoes
7 tablespoons unsalted butter
1 tablespoon oil
Salt
Pepper
6 cloves garlic
1 cup wine vinegar
2 cups chicken bouillon
1 1/2 tablespoons *crème fraîche* or heavy cream
Chervil sprigs

Cooking time: 40 minutes

2 1/2 pounds boneless
braising beef,
such as chuck or shoulder
2 1/4 pounds yellow
onions
5 tablespoons oil
Salt
Freshly ground pepper
3/4 cup good-quality wine
vinegar
4 cups full-bodied red
wine, such as
Côtes-du-Rhône

*Cooking time:
3 hours*

Mariners' Grill

(Grillade marinière)

T*his grillade marinière, which I learned to make and to love when I worked in the kitchen of chef Fernand Point's La Pyramide in Vienne, comes from a tradition-al recipe of the sailors who plied the Rhône river. As every-one knows (or almost everyone), all sailors love to eat and to spend a good long time at the table.*

But since they never know exactly when they will eat, their repertoire of recipes consists largely of long-simmered dishes like this one. Do not worry if it cooks a little longer than indicated. It will not make much difference.

Preheat the oven to 225° F.

Cut the beef into thin slices (or ask your butcher to do this for you). Peel and thinly slice the onions.

Place the oil in a Dutch oven and sprinkle a layer of onions over the bottom. Place a layer of beef slices over the onions, and alternate with another layer of onions and beef slices. Continue in this manner until all the beef and onions are used, ending with a layer of onions.

Season with salt and pepper. Pour the vinegar and wine evenly over the ingredients.

Cover, place in the preheated oven and cook for at least 3 hours.

Serve in the Dutch oven, accompanied by mashed potatoes or small-shell pasta.

Beef on a String

(Bœuf à la ficelle)

All you need for this recipe are flavorful bouillon, a good fillet of beef, and kitchen string. Devised by those who do not like the too-cooked aspect of pot-au-feu, *this is a dish that is not unlike those exotic fondues in which each guest dips his ingredients at will into a simmering bouillon. The difference is that* bœuf à la ficelle *is prepared in the kitchen and arrives at the table neatly cut into rosy-red slices. It has a marvelous taste. But do not confuse it with the* gigot à la ficelle *created (possibly) by Alexandre Dumas. Served in restaurants of the Savoie region, this consists of a leg of lamb hung in an open fireplace and cooked slowly as it turns at the end of a sturdy cord.*

Securely tie up the fillet (as you would a package) with kitchen string, leaving extra lengths of string at each end.

Peel the carrots and celery root (or celery ribs). Cut into 2 by 1/4-inch sticks. Trim and carefully wash the leeks; discard the dark green part. Trim the green beans. Peel the potatoes.

Place the bouillon in a large saucepan and bring to a boil. Add the carrots and celery root and let cook for 5 minutes.

Add the green beans and leeks. When the bouillon returns to a boil, cook for 5 minutes. Correct the seasoning.

Place the potatoes in a saucepan of boiling salted water and cook until fork-tender.

Meanwhile, tie the two loose ends of the string together to form a short loop and slip the handle of a long wooden spoon through the loop so that the fillet can be suspended in the boiling broth when the two ends of the spoon are balanced on the rim of the saucepan. The fillet should be completely covered with bouillon but should not touch the bottom of the pan. If necessary adjust the length of the loop so that the fillet hangs freely in the center of the saucepan. The bouillon should be at a full boil when the fillet is lowered into the saucepan to "seize" the meat and seal in the juices. Reduce heat and cook at a rapid simmer for 10 to 15 minutes per pound.

Remove the meat and the vegetables from the broth. Remove the string, cut the fillet into thick slices and arrange them on a warmed serving platter. Arrange the vegetables and potatoes around the edges.

Serve at once, accompanied by condiments of your choice, including horseradish, coarse salt, mustard, and *cornichons*.

FOR 5 SERVINGS

2 1/4 pounds fillet of beef, rump-steak or other tender cut
8 cups strong vegetable bouillon
3/4 pound carrots
1/4 large celery root (or two ribs celery)
5 leeks
3/4 pound green beans
5 potatoes
Salt
Pepper

Accompaniments:
Horseradish
Coarse salt
Dijon mustard
Cornichons

*Cooking time:
About 20 minutes*

40

FOR 6 SERVINGS

3 to 3 1/2 pounds eye of round
3 cups (1 bottle) red table wine
3 tablespoons marc de Bourgogne or cognac
1 *bouquet garni*
Peppercorns
3 tablespoons oil
5 onions
3 carrots
1/2 pound slab bacon
3 tablespoons unsalted butter
Salt
Freshly ground pepper
1 garlic clove
30 small pearl onions
1 sugar cube

*Cooking time:
2 hours 40 minutes*

Here is a typical example of the common shorthand of the culinary dialect. Needless to say it is not the beef that is bourguignon, but the method of preparing it. A la bourguignonne would be more precise. This preparation, characteristic of the great wine region of Burgundy, includes red wine, onions, mushrooms and bacon.

Cut the beef into 1 to 1 1/2-inch cubes. Place it in a large mixing bowl. Add the wine, marc, *bouquet garni*, a few peppercorns, and 1 tablespoon of the oil. Set aside to marinate for at least 2 hours.

Peel and chop the large onions and the carrots. Remove the rind from the bacon and cut the meat into 1 by 1/4-inch pieces. Plunge the bacon pieces into a saucepan of boiling water and blanch for several seconds. Drain and pat dry.

Remove the beef from the marinade with a slotted spoon and drain on paper towels. Reserve the marinade.

Melt 2 tablespoons of the butter with the remaining oil in a large Dutch oven. Add the bacon and sauté until lightly browned, remove and set aside.

Add the beef to the pan, in two batches if necessary, sauté on all sides, and season with salt and pepper. Remove from the pan.

Add the carrots and onions to the pan and sauté until tender. Return the meat and the bacon to the pan. Add the marinade and *bouquet garni*. Bring to a boil, add the garlic clove (unpeeled but lightly crushed). Cover and simmer over low heat for 2 1/2 hours.

Peel the pearl onions. Melt the remaining butter in a skillet. Add the onions and sauté quickly over medium-high heat without browning. Set aside.

When the meat has finished cooking, remove it and the bacon pieces from the cooking liquid with a slotted spoon. Strain the liquid through a sieve and stir in the sugar cube. Return the sauce to the pan with the meat and the bacon. Add the sautéed pearl onions and warm until sauce, onions and meat are heated through.

Serve with steamed potatoes and croutons sautéed in butter.

Stuffed Breast of Veal

(Poitrine de veau farcie)

When the French word for stuffing—farce—first appeared in the twelfth century, it corresponded to a desire to surprise, to bring to the table more than meets the eye, something richer and more promising.

Stuffed breast of veal (and shoulder) is a much-loved dish in Burgundy. Served warm or cold, cut into thin slices and accompanied with a good garden salad, it is a fitting reward for any hard-working field laborer, and of course, for the rest of us as well.

Make a horizontal cut in the veal breast to hold the stuffing (or ask your butcher to prepare it).

Preheat the oven to 450° F.

To make the stuffing, peel and chop the onions. Rinse, dry and chop the chard leaves.

Melt the butter in a skillet, add the onions and sauté until lightly browned. Add the chard and cook until wilted, stirring with a wooden spoon. Remove from the heat and let cool.

Remove and discard the stems from the parsley. Chop the leaves finely. Peel and chop the garlic.

In a mixing bowl, combine the sausage, ground veal, parsley, garlic, sautéed chard and onion, and mix well.

In a small bowl, beat together the crème fraîche, egg and egg yolk. Add to the mixing bowl with the sausage and veal, season with thyme, salt and pepper. Combine ingredients thoroughly.

Stuff the forcemeat mixture into the pocket of the veal breast, and stitch the opening closed with a barding needle.

Rub the suet generously over the bottom and sides of a baking pan large enough to hold the veal breast. Place the pork rind on the bottom of the pan.

Peel and slice the onions and carrots, and spread them over the rind. Add the bouquet garni.

Place the stuffed veal in the baking pan. Season with salt and pepper. Melt the remaining suet and pour over the veal.

Place in the hot oven and brown, basting occasionally with the bouillon and turning to color equally on all sides. When browned, cover the breast with a piece of buttered parchment paper. Reduce the oven temperature to 325° F., and let cook for 2 hours, adding more bouillon as needed so that the bottom of the baking pan is never dry.

FOR 6 SERVINGS

1 breast of veal, boned (3 to 3 1/2 pounds)
1/4 pound onions
1/2 pound Swiss chard, leaves only, about 5 large leaves (save the stems for an accompanying gratin, if desired)
3 1/2 tablespoons unsalted butter
1 bunch flat-leaf parsley
1 clove garlic
1/4 pound bulk sausage
1/2 pound ground veal
1 egg
1 egg yolk
2 tablespoons crème fraîche or heavy cream
Pinch thyme
Salt
Freshly ground pepper

For the Cooking:
2 ounces suet or bacon fat
1 piece pork rind
2 cups veal stock or bouillon
3 onions
5 carrots
1 bouquet garni
Salt
Freshly ground pepper
2 cups veal bouillon

Special equipment:
1 barding needle
Fine string
Parchment paper

Cooking time:
2 hours 15 minutes

Remove the veal breast from the baking pan and slice thinly.

Arrange on a warmed serving platter.

Deglaze the baking pan with bouillon or water, strain the sauce through a sieve, pour into a sauceboat and pass it with the veal.

Serve with sautéed potatoes or a *gratin* of Swiss chard stems.

43

Boiled Beef and Vegetables

(Pot-au-feu)

The first cook to put "the pot on the fire," as the name of this dish literally means, surely had no idea of the significance of her act. Nor that all the regions of France, or almost all, would claim parenthood for this succulent dish. This stew is from everywhere and nowhere; but every French person has memories of a pot-au-feu like no other. My pot-au-feu à la jambe de bois, for example ("wooden leg" pot-au-feu, the complete recipe I will not give you here, as it is more for a famished brigade than for a normal family), includes beef shin, three veal knuckles, a shoulder of pork, turkey, partridge, leg of lamb, chickens, and truffled sausages. Instead I will offer this recipe for a classic pot-au-feu, one of the simplest and most beautiful creations of French cuisine, and one which I will naturally claim as belonging to the category of typical Lyonnais dishes.

Ask your butcher to prepare the meats as follows: Tie the beef round securely as for roasting. Tie and lard the rump. Cut the oxtail into 1 1/2-inch-thick pieces and tie in a flat pinwheel.

Place the beef ribs in a large stock pot, cover generously with water (about 5 quarts), bring to a boil over medium heat and let cook for about 1 hour, skimming off the foam that rises to the surface.

Peel the onion, stick it with the cloves and add to the stock pot. Peel the carrots and garlic and add. Tie the thyme, parsley, celery rib and bay leaf together and add to the pot.

Return the broth to a boil, add the top round or eye, the rump, and the oxtail, along with peppercorns and a handful of coarse salt. Let simmer gently for 3 hours.

When the meat has cooked (4 hours in all), remove it from the broth and filter the cooking liquid through a fine sieve. Rinse the stock pot, return the meat and the strained liquid to the pan. Bring to a boil and let simmer for 30 minutes.

Wash the leeks thoroughly to remove any sand. Trim off the dark green parts and tie the leeks into small bunches with kitchen string. Peel the baby carrots, turnips, parsnips, and celery root.

Add the carrots, turnips, parsnips and celery root to the simmering broth. Let the liquid return to a boil, boil for 10 minutes, add the leeks and let cook for 20 minutes longer.

FOR 8 SERVINGS

2 pounds top round or eye of round
1 3/4 pounds beef rump
1 oxtail
1 3/4 pounds top beef ribs
8 large slices beef marrow bones
1 1/3 pounds new leeks
2 pounds baby carrots
8 turnips
2 medium-size parsnips
1 small celery root
or 4 ribs celery
8 small new potatoes

For the Cooking:
2 onions
3 cloves
2 carrots
4 cloves garlic
1 sprig thyme
1/2 bunch parsley
1 rib celery
1 bay leaf
15 peppercorns
Coarse salt

Cooking time:
4 1/2 hours

Meanwhile, peel the potatoes and cook them separately in a saucepan of boiling salted water for 20 to 30 minutes.

Fifteen minutes before serving the *pot-au-feu*, dip the ends of the marrow bones in coarse salt and wrap each in a square of cheesecloth. Remove 2 cups of the broth from the pot, place in a saucepan and bring to a boil. Add the marrow bones and poach at a gentle simmer for 10 minutes.

Remove the meats and vegetables from the pot and keep warm. Skim the fat from the top of the cooking liquid and pour the bouillon into a soup tureen.

Slice the meat and arrange it on a warmed serving platter surrounded by the vegetables and the marrow bones.

Serve the bouillon and the condiments (pickles, coarse salt, cherries in vinegar) separately.

Note: A simple method for degreasing the bouillon if it is made in advance is to place it in the refrigerator. The fat rises to the top when chilled and can be lifted off easily before reheating the bouillon.

"Tender and sweet, the parsnip fell out of use for a while, but it has come back into fashion, and any good family pot-au-feu *now includes it, often in lieu of turnips."*

45

Parmentier's Hash

(Hachis Parmentier)

*I*t is often difficult to date recipes, but here is one that definitely appeared after the French Revolution. Antoine Augustin Parmentier, fervent defender and promoter of the potato, a vegetable that was at first widely distrusted by the public, has had his name linked to one of the most famous dishes in the French home cook's repertoire.

This is one of the best reasons for making a pot-au-feu copious enough to stretch over two meals. The leftovers will taste delicious in a hachis parmentier *of chopped beef tucked between two layers of mashed potatoes and lightly browned on top.*

Peel the potatoes and steam or boil them until tender.

Chop the beef. Peel and chop the onions and one of the garlic cloves. Remove the leaves from the parsley, discarding the stems, and chop.

Melt 2 tablespoons of the butter in a skillet. Add the onions and garlic and sauté until transparent. Add the beef and the chopped parsley. Season with the thyme, salt and pepper.

In a small saucepan, bring the milk to a boil. Drain the potatoes, place them in a mixing bowl and mash them to a purée, incorporating the hot milk and 9 tablespoons of the remaining butter cut into small pieces. Press the remaining garlic clove through a garlic press and add to the potatoes. Season with nutmeg, salt, and pepper and beat with a whisk until smooth.

Preheat the oven to 400° F.

Spread a layer of the potatoes over the bottom of a buttered baking dish. Spread a layer of the chopped beef over the potatoes. Continue to alternate the mashed potatoes and chopped beef, ending with a layer of potatoes. Sprinkle the top of the potatoes with the grated cheese and dot with the remaining butter.

Place in the preheated oven and cook for about 20 minutes, until heated through and nicely browned on top.

Serve with a green salad.

Note: The best potatoes for this have a mealy texture and mash easily.

FOR 6 SERVINGS

4 1/2 pound yellow potatoes
1 1/2 pounds boiled beef (such as *pot-au-feu* leftovers)
2 large onions
2 cloves garlic
10 sprigs parsley
13 tablespoons unsalted butter
Pinch ground thyme
Salt
Freshly ground pepper
3/4 cup milk
Pinch grated nutmeg
1 cup grated Gruyère cheese

*Cooking time:
40 minutes*

1 3/4 pounds salted pork
loin or unsmoked ham
1 pound lightly salted
pork ribs
1 small salted pork knuckle
1 1/2 pounds green lentils,
preferably from Puy
1 onion
1 clove
2 carrots
2 cloves garlic
1 rib celery
2 sprigs thyme
1 bay leaf
4 sprigs flat-leaf parsley
Peppercorns
1/3 pound smoked
slab bacon
1 tablespoon suet or
bacon fat
1 Lyon-style pork sausage
(about 1 pound)

Cooking time:
2 1/2 hours

Lentils and Salted Pork

(Petit salé aux lentilles)

As far back as ancient Rome, meat was conserved with salt. And if salting is no longer necessary today to insure against food shortages, it remains a rural tradition in France. Whenever a pig is slaughtered, parts of it go into the salt crock, which in some areas has still not yielded to the invasion of the ubiquitous freezer. What we call petit salé (loin, spareribs, hind knuckle, etc.) sold under the designation demi-sel, must always be desalted before preparation. The time spent in salt tenderizes the meat, so that it requires less cooking than a normal piece of pork. Demi-sel is often used in traditional stews of the Auvergne, like this one featuring the green lentils of Puy (the only lentil to merit an appellation d'origine).

Place the salted pork loin, ribs, and knuckle in a large bowl, add cold water to cover, and let soak for 30 minutes.

Drain and rinse the meats, and place in a large Dutch oven with enough water to cover. Bring to a boil, let simmer gently for 1 hour.

Rinse and drain the lentils, and place in a saucepan with cold water to cover. Bring to a boil and simmer for 10 minutes. Drain.

Once the meats have simmered for an hour, add the drained lentils. Peel the onion and stick it with the clove. Peel the carrots and dice. Add the onion, carrots, and garlic cloves (unpeeled) to the pan.

Tie the celery rib, thyme, bay leaf, and parsley together. Add to the pan along with several peppercorns, let simmer for 50 minutes.

Dice the bacon. Melt the suet in a skillet, add the bacon and sauté. Prick the sausage with a fork.

When the pork has cooked for 50 minutes, add the sausage and cook 10 minutes. Add the sautéed bacon, cook 30 minutes more.

Remove the onion, garlic and *bouquet garni* from the pan.

Remove the meats and cut into pieces. Slice the sausage and arrange on a platter surrounded by the lentils.

Note: If you can not find salted meats, pickled or corned pork or beef can be substituted. Or substitute unsmoked ham for the pork loin, and pre-cook the unsalted pork ribs and knuckle in simmering water seasoned with coarse salt and a bay leaf, for 1 hour before proceeding with the recipe.

Stuffed Cabbage

(Chou farci)

In France, we are certainly blessed with cabbages. I do not know if stuffed cabbage is more indigenous to France than to other countries, but it is, indisputably, very French and very rustic. For best results, choose a dense, well-rounded savoy cabbage of medium size (they appear in the markets in March and April). You will need a little patience and a light touch to keep from breaking the leaves, as well as some string to tie the cabbage back up.

This can easily be served as a one-dish meal.

Soak the caul fat in cold water (if using), drain and rinse several times.

Remove the crusts from the bread and crumble it into a bowl, add the milk and let soak for 5 minutes. Gently squeeze the bread to remove excess liquid, and place the bread in a large mixing bowl.

Finely chop the veal, pork, and bacon separately, or ask your butcher to grind them. Remove the leaves from the parsley and chop them finely.

Peel and chop 2 of the onions. Melt 1 tablespoon of the butter in a skillet, add the chopped onions and sauté until wilted. Add them to the mixing bowl with the bread.

Add the chopped veal, pork, and bacon to the mixing bowl. Add the parsley, egg, and egg yolk. Add the allspice. Season with salt and pepper and mix to blend thoroughly.

Peel and dice the carrots, turnips and the remaining 3 onions.

Bring a saucepan of lightly salted water to a boil. Add the diced carrots, turnips, and onions, and blanch for several minutes.

Refresh the vegetables under cold water. Drain and pat dry.

FOR 8 SERVINGS

1 sheet caul fat (or kitchen string)
5 or 6 slices country-style bread
2/3 cup milk
3/4 pound boned shoulder of veal
3/4 pound pork loin
3/4 pound smoked slab bacon
1 bunch flat-leaf parsley
5 onions
2 1/2 tablespoons unsalted butter
1 egg
1 egg yolk
1/2 teaspoon allspice
Salt
Freshly ground pepper
4 carrots
3 turnips
1 head savoy cabbage
2 cubes chicken bouillon
2 tablespoons vegetable oil

Cooking time:
2 hours 5 minutes

52

Trim the cabbage, removing the tough outer leaves and stem.

Rinse. Blanch it in a large saucepan or stock pot of boiling salted water for about 10 minutes, turning halfway through to cook all sides evenly. Remove the cabbage and rinse under cold water. Drain in a colander, stem side up.

Place the cabbage, stem down, on a work surface. Gently fan out the leaves one by one, being careful not to detach them from the core. Using a sharp knife, remove the inner core or heart.

Preheat the oven to 400° F.

Form two-thirds of the stuffing mixture into a ball the size of the cabbage heart and place in the center of the cabbage. Fold up the inner leaves of the cabbage, wrapping them firmly around the stuffing.

Continue to fold the cabbage leaves around the core, sprinkling the diced vegetables and remaining stuffing mixture between the layers of leaves.

Lay out the caul fat, if using, on a work surface. Place the stuffed cabbage in the center and wrap the fat around it, using kitchen string to tie it firmly but gently in place. Or, use string to gently truss the cabbage.

Dissolve the bouillon cubes in 1 3/4 cups boiling water. Heat the remaining 1 1/2 tablespoons butter with the oil in a large Dutch oven. Add the cabbage and sauté, turning until lightly browned on all sides. Pour the bouillon over the cabbage. Cover and place in the preheated oven to cook for 30 minutes.

Lower the temperature to 300° F. Let cook for 1 1/2 hours more.

3/4 pound long macaroni
1 tablespoon coarse salt
1 truffle (optional)
1 tablespoon unsalted
butter
5 tablespoons grated
Parmesan cheese

For the Sauce:
7 tablespoons unsalted
butter
6 tablespoons flour
2 cups milk
1 teaspoon salt
Pinch freshly ground
pepper
Pinch freshly ground
nutmeg
1/2 cup heavy cream
1 1/2 cups grated Beaufort
or Gruyère cheese

*Cooking time:
About 40 minutes*

Macaroni and Cheese

(Gratin de macaroni)

I have to admit, the Lyonnais did not invent macaroni. Macaroni is a legacy of the Romans who founded our city, and of the Italian presence here in the sixteenth century when Lyon was one of the major economic centers of Europe. The Italians brought the pasta, and we made a gratin *with it. I might add, however, that in this region we have not been won over completely by olive oil. Cream and butter are still our ingredients of choice.*

Fill a large saucepan with 4 quarts of water, add the coarse salt and bring to a boil. Add the macaroni, bring back to a boil and cook for 15 to 20 minutes. Do not overcook; the macaroni should be "al dente." Drain well.

Meanwhile, prepare the sauce: Melt the 7 tablespoons butter in a saucepan, add the flour and mix well. Stir in the milk, salt, pepper, and nutmeg and cook over medium heat, stirring constantly with a whisk until the mixture boils. Let boil briefly. Stir in the cream and about two-thirds of the Beaufort cheese. Continue to cook until the cheese is melted.

Preheat the oven to 400° F.

Finely chop or sliver the truffle, if using. Use the tablespoon butter to coat the bottom and sides of an oval *gratin* dish. Arrange a layer of the macaroni on the bottom of the dish. Spoon a layer of the sauce over, and sprinkle a little of the truffle over the top. Add another layer of macaroni and continue to layer the macaroni, sauce, and truffle in this manner, ending with a layer of sauce. Arrange the remaining Beaufort over the top, and sprinkle evenly with the grated Parmesan.

Place in the preheated oven and cook for 20 minutes until the top is nicely browned.

57

Lyonnais Fritters

(Bugnes)

Like crêpes or waffles, fritters are holiday delicacies that traditionally accompany the festivities of Mardi Gras. Bugnes, little golden pillows often twisted into the form of a figure eight, have been popular since the Middle Ages, when they were sold by itinerant vendors in the same way that waffles are sold today at street fairs. There are also bugnes arlésiennes *(from the city of Arles) and* bugnes *from Burgundy, but the the most famous are indisputably the* bugnes *of Lyon.*

In a mixing bowl, combine the flour and sugar. Add the baking powder and stir until well mixed. Stir in the eggs one at a time.

Add the softened butter, lemon zest and rum and work them into the other ingredients with your fingers until a smooth dough forms.

Place the oil in a large saucepan or deep-fryer and heat, being careful not to let the oil become too hot.

On a lightly floured surface, roll the pastry out until it is quite thin. Using a scalloped pastry wheel, cut the pastry into 4 by 2-inch rectangles, or 4-inch triangles, or rectangles with a slit down the middle through which the corners of the pastry can be pulled to form little bows.

When the oil is hot enough (375° F.), add the dough a few pieces at a time.

As soon as the *bugnes* rise to the surface and are lightly browned all over, remove them with a slotted spoon and place on paper towels to drain.

Sprinkle with the powdered sugar while still warm, and serve.

FOR ABOUT 100 BUGNES

4 cups flour
Pinch sugar
1/2 tablespoon baking powder
4 eggs
1/2 pound unsalted butter, softened
Grated zest of 1 lemon
1 tablespoon rum
8 cups vegetable oil (for frying)
Powdered sugar

Special equipment:
Scalloped pastry wheel

Cooking time:
30 minutes

Pérouges Sugar Cakes

(Galettes au sucre comme à Pérouges)

*T*he galette *is undoubtedly the oldest example of French pastry art. From the* fouace, *a pancake described by Rabelais, to regional sugar cakes associated with seasonal festivities, the list is long indeed. A pastry chef from Pérouges brought this ancient recipe for a butter and sugar cake back into fashion with such success that it is now synonymous with the name of the town itself, like the pralines of Montargis or the* nougat *of Montélimar.*

Remove 8 tablespoons of the butter from the refrigerator in advance and let soften in a warm spot.

Rub the sugar cube over the skin of the lemon until the cube is well saturated with the lemon's oil.

Place the sugar cube in a small bowl, stir in the lukewarm water and sprinkle the yeast over the surface. Let dissolve for 5 minutes.

Place the flour in a large mixing bowl and make a well in the center. Pour the yeast mixture into the well and gradually incorporate enough of the flour from around the edges to make a thick paste. Add the eggs, one by one, incorporating the remaining flour and blending well after each addition. Stir in 4 tablespoons of the sugar, and the salt.

Knead the dough, lifting it, pulling it and slapping it between your hands until well aerated. Add more flour if needed to prevent sticking. Add the softened butter a little at a time, working it into the dough.

Place the dough in a large buttered bowl and cover with a damp cloth. Set aside and let rise in a warm place until doubled in bulk, about 1 hour.

Preheat the oven to 425° F.

Punch down the dough, and knead until smooth and elastic. Divide in half and form into two disks. Place them on a baking sheet covered with parchment paper.

In a small saucepan, melt 5 tablespoons of the remaining butter and brush it over the tops of the *galettes*. Sprinkle the remaining 4 tablespoons granulated sugar evenly over the two *galettes*. Dice the remaining butter into small pieces and divide between the two *galettes*.

Place in the preheated oven and let cook for 15 to 18 minutes.

FOR 2 GALETTES
OF 5 SERVINGS EACH

14 tablespoons unsalted butter
1 sugar cube
1 lemon, washed and dried
1 scant tablespoon yeast (1 envelope)
1/2 cup lukewarm water
3 cups flour
2 eggs
1/2 cup sugar
1 teaspoon salt

Special equipment:
Heavy-duty baking sheets
Parchment paper

*Cooking time:
20-25 minutes*

FOR 8 SERVINGS

1/2 cup milk
1/4 cup unsalted butter
1 cup (8 ounces) solid
(not liquid) honey
2 tablespoons baking soda
2 1/2 cups flour
1/4 star anise
1 clove
1 pinch ground cinnamon
1 pinch ground coriander
1 1/2 teaspoons baking
powder
1/2 cup sugar

Special equipment:
Parchment paper

Cooking time:
50 minutes

Reims, capital of the Champagne region, is the home of French spice bread—it was here that the first professional organization of pain d'épiciers, *or spice bread makers, was founded at the end of the sixteenth century. This bread was, nevertheless, already well known in Dijon as early as the fourteenth century, and the French Revolution catapulted it into a legendary specialty of the city. Though an essentially industrial product today, traditional homemade spice bread is still baked in many French households for special occasions such as Easter, Christmas and New Year's.*

In a small saucepan, warm half of the milk. Add the butter and honey and let them melt. Stir in the baking soda.

Place the flour in a large mixing bowl. Pour the milk and butter mixture over the flour and stir to form a smooth dough. Form into a ball, place in a bowl and cover with a damp cloth. Let rest for 1 hour.

Preheat the oven to 350° F.

Crush the anise and clove with a mortar and pestle until reduced to a powder. Add the anise, clove, cinnamon, coriander, and baking powder to the mixing bowl and knead into the dough.

Line a small loaf pan (about 8 by 3 1/2 by 2 1/4 inches) with buttered parchment paper. Turn the dough into the pan.

Place in the preheated oven and bake for 45 minutes.

Combine the sugar with the remaining 1/4 cup milk and brush generously over the top of the loaf. Return it to the oven for a few seconds.

Turn the spice bread out of the pan and place on a wire rack to cool.

Spice Bread

(Pain d'épices)

61

Pears in Beaujolais

(Poires à la beaujolaise)

The pears I use for this are either Saint-Jean or passe-crassane. The first, small and elongated with very thin skins, arrive in French markets in late June. The second, larger and more rounded, are available from November to May. Both hold up well in cooking. And naturally, the wine I choose is Beaujolais. This pretty dessert, rosy-hued and almost transparent, can be made year-round, served luke-warm or chilled.

Peel the pears carefully, leaving the stems intact.

In a non-reactive saucepan (enamel, stainless steel or lined copper) large enough to hold all the pears, combine the wine, sugar, and orange zest. Break the cinnamon stick and vanilla bean in half and add them to the saucepan. Tie the pepper-corns and clove in a small square of cheesecloth and add.

Bring to a boil and let boil for 5 minutes.

Place the pears in the wine and let cook at a gentle simmer, turning them to coat uniformly with the wine, for 20 minutes.

Remove from the heat and let the pears cool in the wine.

Arrange the fruit in a compote or shallow serving dish.

Stir the *cassis* into the cooled wine syrup and pour over the pears. Serve with macaroons or other crisp cookies.

FOR 6 SERVINGS

12 small spring pears
or 6 large winter pears
3 cups (1 bottle) Beaujolais
wine, preferably Morgon
3/4 cup sugar
Zest of 1 orange,
washed and dried
1 cinnamon stick
1 vanilla bean
6 peppercorns
1 clove
3/4 cup *crème de cassis*
(blackcurrant liqueur)

Cooking time:
30 minutes

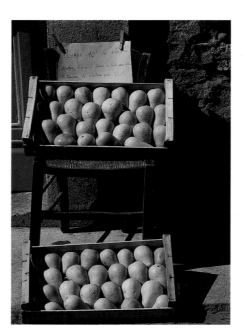

PROVENCE

A hint of garlic and olive oil, the taste of fresh cheeses, the scent of basil, or wild saffron when we can find it, fish in no hurry to come into port ... Provence is all of this. People here take their time, and take the time to say they take their time. The broth for a bouillabaisse can wait a little longer; so can the slow-cooking *daube* that fills the kitchen with its wonderful smell, or the *grand aïoli* that keeps us around the table for hours. All of this is, of course, slightly over-simplified. In this large and fragrant region, the repertoire of dishes is unlimited.

On the coast is the Mediterranean Provence, with its rock fish, its little *favouille* crabs, fried or stuffed squid, sea nettles and the indispensable *rascasses*.

And then there is inland Provence, with its Tricastin truffles, Sisteron lamb, wild *garrigue* rabbits, excellent rice from the Camargue, a multitude of fruits prepared *en confit* in Apt, and goat and sheep cheeses ranging from Brousse to Picodon. It would take too long to name all the products of this region. You will discover some of them in the following pages, prepared in the simplest way to preserve their distinct flavors.

66

Vegetable, Basil and Garlic Soup

(Soupe au pistou)

This is a thick, rich vegetable soup to which pistou, *a mixture of garlic, basil, olive oil and tomatoes, is added at the last moment. The word comes from* pistar, *Provençal for "to grind," since this mixture is traditionally prepared in a mortar and pestle.*

If using dried pinto and white beans, begin soaking them a day in advance. Place them in a large mixing bowl, add enough cold water to cover and let soak overnight. The next day, drain thoroughly.

If using fresh pinto and white beans, they need only be shelled.

Trim and string the green beans and cut into 1/2-inch lengths.

Peel and dice the carrots, potatoes, and onion. Trim off all but the white part of the leek, rinse thoroughly under cold water, and dice. Rinse the zucchini (but do not peel), and dice.

Place the water in a large stock pot, add the pork rind and bring to a boil, skimming off the foam that rises to the top. Season with salt and pepper.

Add the beans and diced vegetables and simmer over low heat for 2 hours.

FOR 6 SERVINGS

1/2 pound fresh or dried pinto beans
1/2 pound fresh or dried white beans
1/2 pound green beans
6 carrots
2 medium potatoes
1 white onion
1 leek
2 zucchini
3 quarts water
1/2 pound pork rind
Salt
Pepper
3 1/2 ounces shell-shaped pasta

For the *Pistou:*
1 pound ripe tomatoes
6 cloves garlic
10 stems basil
Salt
Pepper
3/4 cup olive oil

To serve:
1 1/2 cups grated
Parmesan cheese
1 cup grated Gruyère
cheese

Cooking time:
2 1/2 hours

While the soup cooks, prepare the *pistou:* Peel, seed, and chop the tomatoes and place them in a colander to drain. Peel the garlic, place in a mortar and crush with a pestle. Remove the leaves from the basil, chop and add them to the mortar. Remove a few pieces of the cooked potato from the simmering soup with a slotted spoon, drain and add to the mortar. Work all the ingredients in the mortar together, grinding them with the pestle to obtain a smooth paste. Season with salt and pepper.

Add the olive oil a little at a time, starting with a very thin stream and whisking after each addition until thoroughly incorporated, as for a mayonnaise.

When the mixture is well blended, add the drained tomatoes.

About 15 minutes before the soup has finished cooking, add the pasta and cook until tender.

Turn the hot soup into a soup tureen, removing the pork rind.

Add the *pistou* mixture and mix well. Cover the tureen and let stand for 10 minutes before serving. Place the Parmesan and Gruyère in separate bowls and pass to sprinkle over the soup.

Olive and Caper Spread

(Tapenade)

The name of this dish comes from tapeno, *which means capers in the Provençal dialect. But in addition to capers, this spread includes anchovies, olives, olive oil, and, frequently, lemon.* Tapenade *is excellent as an accompaniment to raw vegetables, meat and fish, or simply as a condiment for potatoes boiled in their skins. Spread on toasted bread, it makes quick canapés for cocktails. It can be kept for about two months stored in a jar, covered with a thin layer of olive oil, and refrigerated.*

Pit the olives. Peel the garlic and remove the pale green stem at the core of the clove (unless using spring garlic, in which case this step is unnecessary).

Place the olives, garlic, anchovies, and capers in a food processor and process with an on-off motion until the mixture is reduced to a paste.

Add the oil slowly and process just until the mixture is smooth and creamy. Store in a jar in the refrigerator covered with a thin film of olive oil.

Serve on toasted slices of country-style bread.

FOR 6 SERVINGS

1 3/4 cups (9 ounces) large black olives, preferably from Nyons
2 cloves garlic
15 to 20 (2 1/2 to 3 ounces) anchovy fillets in olive oil
1/2 cup drained capers
1/2 cup olive oil
Freshly ground pepper

Preparation time: 20 minutes

Anchovy Spread
(Anchoïade)

FOR 6 SERVINGS

25 to 30 (5 1/2 ounces)
anchovy fillets in olive oil
2 cups best quality
virgin olive oil
6 sprigs parsley
8 stems fresh basil
3 cloves garlic
2 tablespoons wine vinegar
Pinch black pepper

*Preparation time:
20 minutes*

Anchovies like the Mediterranean and the Provençaux love anchovies: this is a marriage made in heaven. Anchoïade is a purée of anchovies whisked with olive oil to a creamy consistency. It can be served as a dip for raw vegetables or like Italian "crostini," spread on slices of toasted bread and warmed in the oven.

Drain the anchovies and place them in a skillet with a tablespoon of the oil. Warm over low heat until the anchovies "melt," about 15 minutes.

Place them in a food processor or blender and process to a fine paste.

Remove the leaves from the parsley and basil, discarding the stems, and chop the leaves very finely.

Peel the garlic cloves.

Transfer the anchovy paste to a mortar and add the chopped herbs. Press the garlic through a garlic press and add to the mortar. Stir in the vinegar and mix well.

Work the mixture together with the pestle, incorporating the remaining olive oil little by little, adding it in a very thin stream at first and stirring well after each addition. Season with pepper, mix thoroughly.

Serve the *anchoïade* with a basket of raw vegetables or spread over small tomato halves. It is also delicious with cold meats and toasted bread.

73

Nice-style Salad

(Salade niçoise)

FOR 6 SERVINGS

4 eggs
9 large tomatoes or
18 small plum tomatoes
Salt
1 pound fresh fava beans
1 cucumber
2 green bell peppers
6 spring onions
6 small purple artichokes
12 flat anchovy fillets
1 clove garlic
3/4 cup (3 1/2 ounces)
black *niçoise* or
Mediterranean-style olives
6 stems fresh basil
Freshly ground pepper
1/2 cup olive oil

*Preparation time:
About 20 minutes*

Here is a dish that has suffered so many misinterpretations that it has become something of a catch-phrase, niçoise in name only. In the beginning it included tomatoes, a mixture of wild salad greens known as mesclun, white onions and anchovies. Depending on the season, little artichokes, tender fava beans, and bell peppers might be added. Make sure you include hard-cooked eggs, the famous little black olives from Nice, and a dressing made with a good Mediterranean olive oil. Today tuna, potatoes, rice, and even corn show up in this salad. Why not add lobster and truffles, to boost the price? That would not necessarily be bad, it just would not be niçoise. Nonetheless, the addition of a few fresh green beans, cooked crisp-tender at the last moment, would be acceptable, particularly if you can not find fresh fava beans.

Cook the eggs in a saucepan of boiling salted water for 10 minutes. Rinse immediately under cold water to facilitate peeling. Drain and peel.

Rinse, drain and quarter the tomatoes. Salt lightly.

Shell the fava beans and plunge them into a saucepan of boiling water for 1 minute. Drain and rinse under cold water to refresh, and remove their skins.

Rinse the cucumber and slice into very thin rounds.

Rinse, drain, and seed the peppers. Slice thinly.

Trim the onions and slice thinly. Peel the outer leaves from the artichokes, keeping only the hearts, and cut them into thin slices. Cut the anchovy fillets in thirds.

Cut the garlic clove in half and rub it over the sides and bottom of a salad bowl.

Cut the hard-cooked eggs in quarters. Add them to the salad bowl along with the fava beans, cucumber, peppers, onions, artichokes, anchovy fillets, and olives.

Drain the tomatoes thoroughly, resalt them lightly and drain again. Add them to the salad bowl.

Remove the leaves from the basil and chop them finely. Combine in a small bowl with salt, freshly ground pepper, and olive oil.

Pour this dressing over the salad and toss gently. Chill until ready to serve.

Provençal Flat-Bread with Bacon

(Fougasse aux grattons)

*A*lso called focaccia *in the town of Menton in Southern France, this recipe is, in some respects, more Italian than French. Called* fouaces *or* fougasses *elsewhere, these breads were traditionally sold in the Var region during the Christmas season. Salty or sweet, flavored with bacon-like* grattons*, anchovies, olives or with sugar, today* fougasse *is available year-round. It can be served as a first course or dessert, or with the main dish, like the* galette au lard *of other regions.*

FOR 8 SERVINGS

1/2 pound slab bacon
1 scant tablespoon
(1 packet) active dry yeast
1 cup lukewarm water
3 cups flour
1 tablespoon salt
1 egg yolk

Cooking time:
10 minutes

Dice the bacon, removing any rind. Cook it in a small skillet over medium-high heat until lightly browned. Drain on a paper towel.

In small bowl, sprinkle the yeast over the lukewarm water and let the yeast dissolve.

In a large mixing bowl, combine the flour and the salt. Make a well in the center and add the yeast mixture. With fingertips, gently dust the flour into the center until all the flour is moistened. Work this mixture by hand for about 15 minutes, sprinkling with additional flour if it begins to stick.

Form the dough into a disk, place on a floured surface in a warm place away from drafts. Cut a cross in the top of the dough and let rise for 2 to 3 hours.

Preheat the oven to 500° F.

Incorporate the bacon or *grattons* into the dough, cutting them in with a knife to distribute evenly throughout. Form the dough back into a ball, then begin the cutting process again.

Repeat this operation 2 or 3 times.

Divide the dough into halves. Roll out each half separately, first with a rolling pin, then stretching it by hand to a thickness of about 1/3-inch. Place each sheet of dough on a lightly floured baking sheet. Slash diagonal cuts resembling shafts of wheat over the surface of the dough. The dough will pull away from itself and leave large open sections.

In a small bowl, beat the egg yolk, and brush over the surface of the dough. Place in the preheated oven and cook for about 10 minutes.

Serve warm with a salad.

Provençal Onion Tart
(Pissaladière)

This niçoise *tart derives its name from* pissala, *an ancient local condiment that is a mixture of thyme, bay leaf, cloves, olive oil and puréed anchovies. This condiment is also used for fish and cold meats. The capital of anchovies, salted or in oil, is still Collioure, a beautiful little fortified city in the eastern Pyrenees near the Spanish border.*

If using frozen bread dough, thaw it according to package directions. Spread the dough out on a work surface. Drizzle 2 tablespoons of the oil over it and knead it until the oil is thoroughly incorporated. Roll it into a ball and let it rest. Peel the onions and slice them thinly. Heat 3 tablespoons of the olive oil in a large skillet. Add the onions and *bouquet garni.* Season with salt and pepper and let the onions wilt over medium heat, stirring constantly. They should not brown.

Peel, quarter and seed the tomatoes. Peel and crush the garlic cloves. In a saucepan, heat the remaining tablespoon olive oil. Add the tomatoes, garlic and sugar cube. Season with salt and pepper. Let cook over low heat until reduced to a thick purée.

Preheat the oven to 475° F.

Form the dough into a large disk and flatten to a round about 1/3-inch thick. Roll the edges over to form a small rim and slide the dough onto an oiled baking sheet. Spread the sautéed onions over the dough, discarding the *bouquet garni.* Spread the tomato purée over the top, discarding the crushed garlic. Sprinkle with oregano or marjoram.

Drain the anchovy fillets and arrange them in a crisscross pattern over the top of the tart. Decorate with the olives. Place in the preheated oven and cook for 25 to 30 minutes.

Serve hot or cold.

FOR 6 SERVINGS

2 pounds bread dough
6 tablespoons olive oil
2 1/4 pounds sweet onions
1 *bouquet garni*
Salt
Freshly ground pepper
6 ripe tomatoes
2 cloves garlic
1/2 sugar cube
1 teaspoon ground oregano or
sweet marjoram
25 to 30 (4 1/2 ounces) anchovy fillets in oil
1/3 cup (2 ounces) small black *niçoise* or Mediterranean-style olives

Cooking time:
40 minutes

FOR 4 SERVINGS

1 3/4 pounds salt cod
1 1/4 cup olive oil
1 cup milk
Freshly grated nutmeg
1 tablespoon lemon juice
Truffle slices (optional)

To serve:
Croutons sautéed in butter

Le Cuisinier Durand, *a cookbook published in 1830, includes the authentic recipe for* brandade de Nîmes, *a purée of cod without garlic, even if next door in Marseille they season their version generously with the herb. In fact, I would not be surprised to find a hint of garlic flavoring the* brandade *made today in households surrounding Nîmes's famous Roman arena. There are many other versions, some including anchovies and potatoes, and others without either garlic or milk. In any case, this versatile fish, traditionally reserved for the Lenten season, is rarely considered a solemn dish.*

Begin soaking the cod a day in advance. Place it, skin side up, in a colander set in a large basin of cold water and soak for 12 to 24 hours, changing the water several times. If possible, place in the sink under a trickle of constantly running water for several hours.

Cut the cod in half. Place it in a large saucepan and add enough cold water to cover. Bring slowly to a boil and let simmer for a few minutes, skimming off the foam that rises to the top.

Remove the cod and drain. Remove the skin and bones. Keep warm.

In two separate saucepans, heat the oil and the milk.

Flake and purée the cod, either by placing it in a mortar and mashing with a pestle or by processing briefly in a food processor.

Incorporate the hot oil and milk a little at a time, alternating the two. The *brandade* should not be too runny nor too stiff, and its texture should be fine.

Add a pinch of nutmeg and about a tablespoon of lemon juice.

Stir in the truffle slices, if using.

Serve the *brandade* at room temperature accompanied by the croutons.

Provençal Fish Stew

(Bouillabaisse)

There must be as many authentic bouillabaisse recipes as there are Provençal cooks, and every attempt to narrowly define this recipe has failed. So, let us accept it for what it is—an excellent fish stew more or less rich in fish, depending on the catch of the day, and seasoned to taste with saffron. For me, the only unalterable rule is that this dish be served in two courses: the broth and the fish separately, and accompanied by a rouille or, as some people prefer, an aïoli.

Rinse the soup fish in cold water, do not scale them.

Peel the onions and garlic. Trim the leeks, reserving white parts only, and rinse thoroughly under cold water. Cut the leeks into large rounds and chop the onions. Mash the garlic. Trim and chop the fennel. Core, seed and coarsely chop the tomatoes. Peel the potatoes and cut them into thick rounds.

Heat 3 tablespoons of the oil in a large, heavy-bottom soup kettle or stock pot. Add the onions and leeks and cook over medium-high heat until wilted. Add the fennel, tomatoes, crushed garlic, parsley, thyme, and bay leaf. Let simmer for 10 minutes.

Season with salt and pepper, and add the dried red pepper and orange peel. Let cook for 15 minutes, pressing ingredients down with the back of a wooden spoon to mash them into a coarse, mealy consistency.

Add 3 quarts boiling water, pushing ingredients down firmly, and let boil for 1 hour.

Meanwhile, prepare the *Rouille*:

Cook the potato in a small saucepan of boiling salted water until tender. Drain.

Peel the garlic cloves and place them in a large mortar. Add the dried red pepper, salt, pepper and saffron. Crush the ingredients with a pestle to obtain a coarse paste. Add the potato and crush until thoroughly incorporated. Add the olive oil in a very thin trickle at first, whisking constantly as if making a mayonnaise until the oil is absorbed. Set aside.

Remove the fennel ribs, thyme, bay leaf, dried red pepper and orange peel from the stock pot.

Pass the soup through a food mill fitted with a large-hole grid, then strain through a fine sieve, pressing firmly with the back of a wooden spoon to extract all the juice. Stir in the saffron and correct the seasoning. Rinse the stock pot.

FOR 8 TO 10 SERVINGS

3 1/2 pounds "soup" fish (see note)
3 medium onions
6 cloves garlic
2 medium leeks
1 medium fennel bulb
6 medium tomatoes
8 to 10 small potatoes
1/3 cup olive oil
6 sprigs flat-leaf parsley
1 sprig thyme
1/2 bay leaf
Salt
Freshly ground pepper
1 small dried red pepper, crushed
1 1-inch piece orange peel
3 quarts boiling water
1 pinch saffron threads
6 1-inch pieces monkfish
3 1-inch-thick slices of hake or halibut
6 1-inch slices of eel
4 small trout, cleaned
3 pounds red snapper
2 1/4 pounds John Dory or sea bass
6 small blue crabs, cleaned and rinsed
1 to 2 loaves crusty French-style bread

For the *Rouille*:
1 large potato
6 cloves garlic
1 dried red pepper, crushed
Salt
Freshly ground pepper
1/8 teaspoon saffron threads
1 2/3 cups olive oil

Cooking time for the soup: 2 1/4 hours

Place the potato rounds in the bottom of the stock pot. Add the soup and place over medium heat. Let cook for 5 minutes. Add the remaining fish, the large and firm-fleshed varieties first, to poach in the soup for about 10 minutes: start with the monkfish and let it poach briefly before adding the hake or halibut, eel, and trout, and finally the snapper and John Dory or sea bass.

Heat the remaining oil in a large skillet, add the crabs and sauté quickly over high heat.

Preheat the oven to 400° F.

Slice the bread into 1/2-inch slices, and place on a baking sheet in the preheated oven to dry. Remove from the oven and when cool enough to handle, rub the cut side of the remaining garlic clove over the top of each bread round.

Remove the fish from the soup and arrange on a warmed serving platter with the crabs. Pour the hot soup into a tureen.

Arrange the bread rounds on a separate platter. Pass the *rouille* in the mortar.

Note: Any firm-fleshed, lean white fish such as whiting, cod, bass, flounder, haddock or eels with heads and tails will work well in this recipe.

81

Rougets de Roche with Basil

(Petits rougets de roche au pistou)

*T*here is a recipe for red mullets from Brittany that are *sautéed in salted butter and quickly turn a bright red. They are close cousins of another red mullet, the Mediterranean* rouget de roche, *but they are only cousins. In any case, whether from the north or the south, the first quality to look for in a* rouget *is freshness. I prepare them here* à la nage, *meaning in an aromatic stock, accompanied by a mixture of crushed basil and olive oil.*

Peel the carrots and onions, slice them into thin rounds. Peel and crush the garlic. Rinse, trim and chop the fennel and celery.

Place 1 1/2 tablespoons olive oil in a saucepan over low heat.

Add the garlic, carrots, onions, fennel, and celery and let cook, stirring constantly, for 10 minutes. Sprinkle the *pastis* over and let evaporate for 1 minute. Add 3/4 cup of the wine and let reduce by half. Add 3/4 cup more wine and let reduce by half again. Add the remaining wine and let reduce by half.

Add the water, thyme, salt, and a few peppercorns and let cook for 10 minutes. Remove from the heat and let cool to lukewarm.

Rinse the *rougets* under cold water without gutting them. Dry them.

Transfer the *nage* or stock to a deep-sided, heavy-bottom skillet. Bring to a simmer over medium heat. Add the fish to the skillet, cover and let cook for 3 minutes.

Remove from the heat and let cool to nearly lukewarm in the stock, uncovered.

Peel the garlic and place it in a food processor or blender with the basil leaves and a pinch of coarse salt and process, adding the oil little by little. Season with pepper.

Gently lift the warm *rougets* from the stock with a slotted spoon and place them on a shallow serving platter. Pour the basil and garlic sauce over them and serve.

FOR 6 SERVINGS

For the *Nage*:
3 medium carrots
5 small white pearl
or spring onions
2 cloves garlic
1 small fennel rib
1 small celery rib
1 1/2 tablespoons olive oil
Few drops *pastis* or
Pernod, an anise-
flavored liqueur
2 cups dry white wine
1 1/4 cups water
1 sprig thyme
Pinch coarse salt
A few peppercorns

For the *Rougets*:
18 small *rougets de roche*
or small red mullets
1 clove garlic
20 leaves fresh basil
Coarse salt
1/2 cup virgin olive oil
Freshly ground pepper

Cooking time:
Court-bouillon, *30 minutes*
Rougets, *3 minutes*

84

Cod and Vegetables with Garlic Mayonnaise

(Grand aïoli)

Aïoli, *dubbed "the butter of Provence," is a strong garlic mayonnaise prepared in a mortar. A* grand aïoli, *on the other hand, is a meal in itself, composed of fresh, steamed vegetables, hard-cooked eggs, snails and cod, all accompanied by the* aïoli. *Seasonal products can be included, such as asparagus, fennel, small purple artichokes from Provence, and other fish varieties. Everything is cooked in a* court-bouillon *and diners help themselves according to their taste. The* aïoli *can be served in the mortar.*

Start soaking the cod a day in advance. Place it in a colander set in a basin of cold water and let soak overnight.

The next day, prepare the *court-bouillon*: Peel the carrot and onion and stick the onion with the cloves. Peel the garlic. Trim and thoroughly wash the leek. Place these vegetables in a large stock pot with the *bouquet garni* and the water. Season with salt and pepper.

Bring slowly to a boil, skimming off the foam that rises to the surface, and let simmer for 30 minutes. Remove from the heat and let cool.

Add the snails to the cooled *court-bouillon*. Bring to a boil and let simmer for 20 minutes. Remove and drain the snails.

Cook the eggs in a saucepan of boiling water for 10 minutes. Rinse immediately under cold water and peel.

Cut the stems from the artichokes at the base, and peel off about two-thirds of their leaves. Rinse and cook for 10 minutes in salted boiling water acidulated with the lemon juice. Drain.

Trim and rinse the cauliflower and separate it into flowerets.

Cook in a saucepan of boiling salted water for 8 minutes. Drain.

Peel the potatoes, carrots, and onions. Trim the green beans.

Rinse the zucchini, but do not peel. Cook the potatoes in boiling salted water until tender. Cook the other vegetables separately in boiling salted water until just tender but still slightly crunchy or "al dente," and drain.

Rinse the cod again thoroughly in cold water. Place about 2 cups of the *court-bouillon* in a deep-sided skillet or saucepan. Add the cod and poach for about 8 minutes at a gentle simmer.

FOR 6 SERVINGS

2 3/4 pounds dried salt cod
3 dozen snails (*petit gris*, if possible)
6 eggs
6 small purple artichokes
1 tablespoon lemon juice
1 small cauliflower (1 3/4 pounds)
2 1/4 pounds new potatoes
1 1/2 pounds baby carrots
2 1/4 pounds white onions
1 1/3 pounds small green beans
1 1/3 pounds small zucchini
Salt
Freshly ground pepper

For the *Court-bouillon*:
1 carrot
1 onion
2 cloves
4 cloves garlic
1 leek
1 *bouquet garni* (fennel, celery, parsley, thyme, bay leaf)
6 cups water
Salt
Freshly ground pepper

For the *Aïoli*:
6 cloves garlic
1 egg yolk
Salt
1 2/3 cups olive oil
Juice of 1/2 lemon
Freshly ground pepper

Cooking time:
About 1 hour

To make the *aïoli*: Peel the garlic cloves, place them in a mortar and crush with the pestle until reduced to a paste. Add the egg yolk and season with salt. Gradually incorporate the olive oil, adding it in a very thin stream at first and stirring constantly with a wooden spoon. Stir in the lemon juice and season with pepper.

Arrange the cod, the snails and the hard-cooked eggs, cut in half lengthwise, in the center of a large serving platter and surround them with the vegetables.

Serve the *aïoli* sauce on the side in its mortar.

Provençal Beef Stew

(Daube de bœuf à la provençale)

There is always enough time for everything in Provence. *The sun shines all day long and the* daube *simmers slowly. Four or even six hours of cooking—enough time to include a little siesta.* Daube *is a method of cooking* à l'étouffée, *meaning slow cooking in a* daubière, *a pot with a cover designed to hold hot water. Traditionally placed in a hearth, the* daubière *heats from above and below. When the soldier in one of French author Jean Giono's novels comes upon an inn, he finds it sacked and abandoned, except for the* daube *still on the fire, cooking gently.*

Begin a day in advance.

The day before, cut the meat into large cubes. Prepare the vegetables for the marinade: Trim and chop the celery. Peel and chop the onion, carrots, and shallots. Peel the garlic.

Place the meat in a large bowl with the chopped vegetables and whole garlic cloves. Add the parsley, savory, bay leaves, orange zest, wine, cognac, and oil. Let marinate, refrigerated, for 12 hours.

The next day, blanch the calf's foot and the pork rind in a large saucepan of salted boiling water for 5 minutes. Drain and rinse under cold water. Dice the calf's foot.

Chop the slab bacon and fatback into 1 by 1/4-inch pieces, removing any rind. Chop the parsley finely and roll the fatback in it.

Prepare the vegetables: Peel and finely chop the carrots and onions. Peel and crush the garlic. Chop the celery heart. Peel, seed and quarter the tomatoes.

Remove the meat from the marinade with a slotted spoon and drain it on paper towels. Strain the marinade through a fine sieve.

Preheat the oven to 250° F.

Heat the oil in a large skillet and sauté the meat over high heat until lightly browned. Season with salt and pepper.

Place the pork rind in the bottom of a large Dutch oven or earthenware casserole. Spread about 1/3 of the meat over the rind. Add about 1/3 of the chopped vegetables, and sprinkle with some of the bacon, fatback, and diced calf's foot. Continue to layer the ingredients in this manner until all are used.

FOR 8 SERVINGS

1 1/3 pounds top
or bottom round
of beef
1 1/3 pounds chuck
or shoulder of beef
1 1/3 pound beef cheeks
1 calf's foot, soaked and
boned
1 piece pork rind
1/2 pound slab bacon
1/4 pound fatback
1/2 bunch parsley
4 carrots
3 onions
3 cloves garlic
1 celery heart
3 tomatoes
2 tablespoons olive oil
1 *bouquet garni*
(thyme, bay leaf, parsley,
savory)
Zest of 1 orange
1 tablespoon peppercorns
1 pinch allspice
Flour
Salt

For the Marinade:
1 celery rib
1 onion
2 carrots
3 shallots
3 cloves garlic
1/2 bunch parsley
1 sprig savory
2 bay leaves
Zest of 1 orange
3 cups red wine,
preferably Gigondas
6 tablespoons cognac
3 tablespoons olive oil

*Cooking time:
5 1/2 hours*

Add the *bouquet garni*, orange zest, peppercorns (tied in a square of cheesecloth) and the allspice. Add the strained marinade.

Prepare a moist dough of flour and water, form it into a long cord and place it around the rim of the pan. Moisten the edge of the pan, cover with warm water and press it down firmly on the dough to form a seal.

Place in the preheated oven and bake for 5 hours. Remove from the oven, break the flour crust and remove the cover. Turn the oven off, and return the *daube* to the oven to rest, uncovered, in the residual heat for 30 minutes longer.

Serve with fresh pasta.

Navarin of Spring Lamb

(Navarin d'agneau printanier)

A delicate version of mutton stew, this is a ragoût characterized by the tender spring vegetables it contains. It is, therefore, printanier, or a springtime navarin. It could easily be attributed to any region of France where one finds lamb and turnips, but I have included it in Provence because of the lamb of Sisteron and the Alpilles, which is raised in the fresh air and is redolent of the herbs on which it grazes. This earthy dish might owe part of its name to the victory of Navarin in Greece (1827). That is one theory. Or is it called navarin simply because of the navets (turnips) included in the ingredients?

Cut the shoulder, neck and breast of lamb into 2-inch pieces.

Peel, seed, and chop the tomatoes. Peel and crush the garlic cloves.

Heat 1 1/2 tablespoons of the oil in a Dutch oven or large saucepan, add some of the lamb pieces and sauté over medium-high heat until browned on all sides. Remove and set aside.

Continue to sauté the remaining lamb in small quantities, adding a little more oil if necessary, until all has been browned. Add the garlic and let cook for a minute or two longer.

Pour off two-thirds of the fat that remains in the pan. Return the lamb to the pan, sprinkle evenly with the flour and cook over high heat for a minute or two to dry the meat slightly. Add the chopped tomatoes and season with salt and pepper.

Warm the stock in a small saucepan and pour over the lamb. Add the bouquet garni and bring to a boil. Cover and let simmer over medium-low heat for about 30 minutes.

Peel the onions and carrots. Peel and quarter the turnips.

Add the onions, carrots and turnips to the lamb and let simmer 30 minutes longer.

Meanwhile, rinse and drain the snow peas. Place in a saucepan of boiling salted water and let cook, uncovered, for 8 minutes.

Drain, rinse briefly under cold water, and add to the lamb 3 minutes before ready to serve.

Remove the bouquet garni and serve.

FOR 6 SERVINGS

1 3/4 pounds lamb shoulder
1 3/4 pounds lamb neck
1 3/4 pounds breast of lamb
3 tomatoes
3 cloves garlic
2 to 3 tablespoons oil
1 tablespoon flour
Salt
Freshly ground pepper
3 cups lamb or beef stock
1 bouquet garni
2 bunches spring onions
2 bunches baby carrots
2 bunches baby turnips
1 pound snow peas

Cooking time:
1 hour 10 minutes

Stuffed Vegetables

(Petits farcis)

One of the most pleasing inventions of Provençal cuisine is the art of dressing up garden and market vegetables by stuffing them with *daube* or *pot-au-feu leftovers*, or with rice, bread, herbs and other vegetables to make a meatless stuffing. Count on four or five peppers per person if you are serving them as a main course.

Preheat the oven to 350° F.

For the Peppers:

Rinse the peppers. Core, seed and chop 2 of them. Peel and chop the onions. Peel and chop the garlic.

Chop the slab bacon as finely as possible, removing any rind.

Heat 2 tablespoons of the olive oil in a skillet. Add the onions and sauté until wilted. Remove and set aside. Add the bacon and cook, stirring, until lightly browned. Remove and set aside. Add the rice to the skillet and cook, stirring with a wooden spoon until all the grains are well coated with the fat remaining in the skillet.

Return the onions and bacon to the skillet. Add the chopped peppers and garlic. Add the boiling water and cook over medium heat for 20 minutes. Remove from the heat and let cool slightly.

When cooled, stir in the eggs and Parmesan. Remove the leaves from the basil, chop finely and add to the mixture. Season with salt and pepper.

Rinse the remaining 6 peppers. Remove the stems and slice off the tops. Core them and remove the seeds from the top, being careful not to break the shell. Fill each pepper with the stuffing. Place them on an oiled baking sheet.

Place in the preheated oven and let cook for 30 minutes, turning them halfway through the cooking.

For the Tomatoes:

Rinse and drain 6 of the tomatoes. Remove the stems and slice the tops off horizontally, reserving the tops. Scoop out the seeds and pulp. Sprinkle the interior lightly with salt and invert on a wire rack to let the tomatoes drain.

Peel and chop the onions. Peel and chop the garlic.

Rinse, drain and chop the chard. Peel, seed and chop the 2 remaining tomatoes.

FOR 6 SERVINGS

For the Peppers:
8 bell peppers, red, yellow or green
2 onions
1 clove garlic
1/2 pound slab bacon
2 tablespoons olive oil
2/3 cup rice
1 2/3 cups boiling water
2 eggs, beaten
1/2 cup grated Parmesan cheese
3 sprigs fresh basil
Salt
Freshly ground pepper

Cooking time:
1 hour

For the Tomatoes:
8 medium tomatoes, ripe but firm
Salt
2 onions
1 clove garlic
5 large Swiss chard leaves (about1/2 pound)
4 tablespoons olive oil
1/4 pound ground beef
1/4 pound ground pork
2 ounces ground veal
2 eggs, beaten
3/4 cup grated Parmesan cheese
Freshly ground pepper

Cooking time:
1 hour

Heat 2 tablespoons of the olive oil in a skillet. Add the onion and cook until wilted. Add the tomatoes, chard, garlic, ground beef, ground pork, and ground veal. Cook, stirring, over medium heat for 15 minutes. Let cool.

Stir in the eggs and Parmesan, correct the seasoning and mix until thoroughly combined.

Spoon this stuffing into the drained tomatoes. Place them in an oiled *gratin* dish and drizzle with the remaining olive oil.

Replace the tops on the tomatoes.

Place in the preheated oven and cook for 30 minutes.

For the Eggplants:

Peel and quarter the onion. Peel the garlic cloves.

Rinse the eggplants and remove their stems. Cook in a saucepan of boiling water with the onion and 1 garlic clove for 8 to 10 minutes. Run the eggplants under cold water, drain, and pat dry.

Cut the eggplants in half lengthwise and scoop out the flesh with a teaspoon, reserving the flesh and being careful not to pierce the skin.

Chop the bacon, removing any rind. Rinse and drain the anchovies.

Heat 2 tablespoons of the olive oil in a skillet, add the bacon and sauté, stirring, over medium heat. Add the anchovies and let them warm and "melt" gently over medium heat. Remove from the heat and let cool.

Stir in the egg, breadcrumbs, Parmesan and the reserved eggplant flesh. Mix thoroughly.

Spoon this stuffing into the eggplant halves and place them on an oiled baking sheet or *gratin* dish.

Chop the basil leaves and the remaining garlic clove. Add them to the tomato purée along with the cayenne. Spoon this mixture over the eggplants. Drizzle with the remaining 2 tablespoons olive oil.

Place in the preheated oven and cook for 45 minutes.

For the Zucchini:

Place the rice in a saucepan of boiling salted water and cook for 20 minutes. Drain.

Peel and chop the onion. Chop the bacon, removing any rind.

Rinse the zucchini, cut them in half lengthwise and scoop out the flesh with a spoon, being careful not to pierce the skin. Chop the zucchini flesh.

Heat the olive oil in a skillet, add the onions and cook until wilted. Add the zucchini flesh. In a mixing bowl, combine the rice, onions, and zucchini flesh. Add the chopped bacon, eggs, and Parmesan cheese and mix thoroughly.

Peel the garlic. Chop the garlic and basil leaves together and add them to the stuffing.

For the Eggplants:
1 onion
2 cloves garlic
3 large eggplants
2 ounces slab bacon
2 anchovy fillets
4 tablespoons olive oil
1 egg, beaten
1 tablespoon fresh breadcrumbs
1/2 cup grated Parmesan cheese
3 stems fresh basil
1/2 cup fresh tomato purée
Pinch cayenne pepper
Salt
Freshly ground pepper

Cooking time:
About 1 hour

For the Zucchini:
1/3 cup rice
1 medium onion
2 ounces cooked slab bacon
6 medium zucchini
2 tablespoons olive oil
2 eggs, beaten
1 cup grated Parmesan cheese
1 clove garlic
2 stems fresh basil
1 tablespoon breadcrumbs
Salt
Freshly ground pepper

Cooking time:
1 hour 10 minutes

For the Onions:
6 small medium onions
1/3 cup rice
1/4 cup olive oil
2 ounces cooked slab bacon
2 eggs, beaten
1 cup grated Parmesan cheese
1 clove garlic
2 sprigs fresh basil
1 tablespoon breadcrumbs

Cooking time:
About 1 hour

Spoon the stuffing into the zucchini halves. Sprinkle them with the breadcrumbs.

Place them on an oiled baking sheet and cook in the preheated oven for 40 minutes.

For the Onions:

Peel the onions and cook them in a saucepan of boiling salted water for 15 minutes. Drain and pat dry.

Slice off the tops of the onions and scoop out all but about 2 layers of the interior flesh of each, reserving the flesh.

Cook the rice in boiling salted water for 20 minutes.

Chop the reserved onion flesh. Place it in a skillet with 2 tablespoons of the olive oil and and cook until wilted.

Chop the bacon finely, removing the rind, and place in a mixing bowl with the cooked rice and onions. Stir in the eggs and the Parmesan cheese.

Peel the garlic and chop finely with the basil leaves. Add to the mixing bowl and blend thoroughly.

Spoon this mixture into the scooped-out onions. Place them on an oiled baking sheet or *gratin* dish. Sprinkle with the breadcrumbs and drizzle with the remaining olive oil.

Cook in the preheated oven for 35 minutes.

Fresh Cheese Tart

(Tarte au brocciu)

Although originally from Corsica, this dish is also made in Provence, where brocciu *(fresh sheep cheese) is called* brousse.

This is a light cheesecake that you will not find in the summer months, since brocciu *is available only from autumn to the beginning of spring.*

Brocciu *or* brousse *is also used in omelettes, and I have a vivid memory of a* brocciu *omelette prepared by a woman dressed all in black, near a mountain stream above the ancient Corsican city of Calvi.*

Preheat the oven to 475° F.

Using a sharp knife, remove and chop the lemon peel.

Place the *brocciu* in a mixing bowl and mash with a fork.

In a separate mixing bowl combine the eggs and sugar, and beat until the mixture is smooth and a light lemon yellow. Pour it over the *brocciu* and mix thoroughly. Stir in the chopped lemon.

Thoroughly butter the bottom and sides of a deep-sided 9-inch quiche pan. Place in the center of the preheated oven. Reduce the temperature to 300° F. and cook for 45 minutes.

Serve hot or cold.

FOR 6 SERVINGS

1 lemon, washed and dried, or
1/2 cup *eau-de-vie*
16 ounces (2 cups) *brocciu*, or fresh goat cheese
5 eggs
1 1/3 cup sugar
1 tablespoon butter

Special equipment:
1 9-inch, deep-sided quiche mold

Cooking time:
45 minutes

Swiss Chard Tourte

(Tourte aux blettes)

FOR 6 SERVINGS

Pastry:
2 cups flour
1/2 cup sugar
2 eggs, beaten
Pinch salt
8 tablespoons unsalted
butter, softened

Filling:
1/3 cup raisins
3 tablespoons rum
1 pound Swiss chard leaves
(about 6 cups,
loosely packed)
1 cup loosely-packed
brown sugar
1 egg, beaten
1/3 cup pine nuts
1/4 cup whole, blanched
almonds, ground to
a powder
1 teaspoon olive oil
Pinch pepper
3 apples
1 tablespoon sugar,
for dusting

Cooking time:
30 minutes

*C*hard, *called* blettes *or* bettes *in French, is a vegetable prized for its leaves—they are bright green and, like spinach, are used in* hachis *and stuffings to add a touch of color. Typically Provençal, this* tourte aux blettes *is a classic vegetable tart that makes the most of the fresh produce of the region. Here is a sweet version that can be eaten warm or cold.*

Prepare the pastry 1 hour in advance. To do so, place the flour in a large mixing bowl, make a well in the center and add the sugar, eggs, and salt. Cut the butter into pieces and add to the flour. Mix together quickly with the fingertips.

Work the dough by hand until blended and crumbly. Roll into a ball and place in the refrigerator to rest for 1 hour.

Preheat the oven to 400° F.

For the filling, place the raisins in a small bowl with the rum to plump. Trim, rinse and dry the chard leaves. Cut into strips. Plunge them into a saucepan of boiling water and let blanch for 1 minute. Drain the leaves and spread out on paper towels to dry. Drain the raisins.

In a mixing bowl, combine the brown sugar, egg, drained raisins, pine nuts, almond powder, oil and pepper. Stir in the chard leaves.

Divide the pastry into 2 unequal parts, one-third and two-thirds. Form into balls and roll each ball out into a disk.

Line the bottom and sides of a buttered 9 to 10-inch pie pan (preferably with removable bottom) with the larger pastry disk. Turn the filling into the pastry shell.

Peel, core and slice the apples. Arrange the apple slices evenly over the filling.

Place the second pastry sheet on top. Moisten the rims of the top and bottom pastry sheets and press edges firmly together to seal. Prick the top of the tart with the tines of a fork.

Place in the center of the preheated oven and bake for 30 minutes.

Remove from the oven and sprinkle the top of the *tourte* with the sugar while still hot.

Serve warm or cold.

97

BORDELAIS

nder the Bordelais heading, I have included a good part of the Aquitaine, as well as some specialties from the Basque country, even if this latter deserves a chapter of its own. It seems to me that the Bordeaux region has *everything* to gain by association with its southwestern neighbors. Despite its powerful and unique position in the world, Bordeaux is not a gastronomic bellwether. The region's brilliance is concentrated in its wines, even though quality products are no rarer here than elsewhere, and surrounding provinces supply anything that might be lacking, including *foie gras* and

confit, the tender lamb of Pauillac and the butter of Charentes. There are some typically Bordelais traditions that are nonetheless notable, such as the habit of serving oysters accompanied by sausages and grilled *crepinettes*, little sausage patties encased in caul fat. There is the famous *lamproie à la bordelaise*, a fresh- and saltwater fish resembling eel that is traditionally cooked in its own blood, and the *pibales*, the famous baby eels that are served fried or fricasseed. And, of course, the châteaux have a long, rich tradition of bourgeois cooking, but here again, it is most often a foil for the excellent Bordeaux wines, as if the food was simply an accompaniment. It is for this reason that I have turned to the Béarnais, the Gascons, and the Basques for a little assistance. While keeping their own identity, each of the above contributes to reinforcing the image of a gastronomic Southwest that definitely knows its way around a table.

Cabbage Soup

(Garbure)

This is certainly not a fashionably thin soup. It is full of good things, including slab bacon, preserved duck (and sometimes sausages and pork knuckle), and is a meal in itself. But there are other versions: garbure à l'oignon, *the Lyonnais interpretation (with onions, of course) of the only authentic* garbure, *that from the Béarn region. A good* garbure *should be thick enough to hold up a spoon. At least that is what they say in Pau.*

FOR 8 SERVINGS

For the Bouillon:
3 carrots
2 turnips
1 onion
2 ribs celery
2 leeks
1 chicken
Coarse salt
A few peppercorns
4 quarts cold water

Other ingredients:
1 small savoy cabbage
1 3/4 pounds potatoes
1 pound carrots
1 pound shelled fresh
white beans (see note)
1 pound *confit* of gizzards
(see note)
1 1/4 pound *confit* of
goose wings with their fat
(see note)
1/2 pound slab bacon
1 clove garlic
Salt
Pepper

*Cooking time:
At least 3 hours*

Peel the carrots, turnips, and onion. Rinse and trim the celery ribs and leeks. Place them in a large stock pot with the chicken, a pinch of coarse salt and the peppercorns. Cover with the water and bring to a boil. Let simmer for 2 hours. Remove the chicken and vegetables from the broth, and reserve for another use. Reserve the broth.

Peel the outer leaves from the cabbage and discard. Cut the cabbage in quarters. Plunge them into a saucepan of boiling salted water and boil for 10 minutes, drain. Peel and rinse the potatoes, and cut them in quarters. Peel the carrots and chop them coarsely. Cook the beans in boiling salted water for 45 minutes. Spread a little fat from the preserved gizzards and goose wings over the cabbage quarters.

Coarsely chop the bacon. Peel the garlic. Place the chicken broth in a large stock pot. Add the bacon and the garlic clove. Let simmer for 20 minutes, then add the cabbage, potatoes, and carrots, and let cook for 30 minutes.

Add the beans, gizzards and wings. Let cook for 1 hour at a gentle simmer. Correct the seasoning, if necessary, and serve very hot.

Note: If fresh beans are not available, substitute dried beans that have been soaked overnight in cold water.

Confit, the traditional method of preserving meats by simmering them slowly in fat, then storing them in a cool place, adds a special flavor to this soup. *Confits* of duck and gizzards are exported and can often be found in jars or cans in specialty food stores. But if you wish to make your own, follow the recipe on page 144, substituting gizzards and goose (or turkey) wings for the thighs and breast.

FOR 4 SERVINGS

2 1/4 pounds salt cod
3 sweet peppers
1 dried red pepper
1 2/3 pounds sweet onions
4 cloves garlic
3 sprigs parsley
2 ounces raw-cured ham
such as Parma ham
1 2/3 cups olive oil
1/4 pound ham fat
1 butter biscuit or zwieback
2 tablespoons tomato
sauce
1/2 tablespoon butter
Salt
Pinch white pepper
Pinch cayenne

*Cooking time:
Cod, 15 minutes
Sauce, 2 1/4 hours*

Biscay is one of the Basque provinces of Spain, but the adjective biscayenne frequently applies to dishes found on the other side of the Spanish border, in France. It was in the Basque village of Saint-Jean-Pied-de-Port that I had the privilege of tasting Arrambide cod, some of the best in the world. The preparation of the sauce takes a little time, but since the cod needs to be soaked for least 24 hours, you can prepare the sauce the day before.

A day in advance, bone the cod without removing the skin. Cut it into 4 pieces, and place them skin side up in a colander set in a large basin of cold water. Let soak for 24 hours, changing the water frequently.

The next day, rinse the cod. Scrape off the skin. Pat the fish dry. Set aside.

Soak the sweet peppers and dried red pepper in a bowl of hot water for 2 hours. Drain and cut them open to remove the core, stem and seeds. Peel the onions and 1 clove garlic and chop finely. Tie the parsley sprigs together. Chop the ham into small pieces.

Heat 2/3 cup of the oil in a skillet. Add the chopped onions and garlic, parsley, ham, and ham fat. Crumble the biscuit and add to the skillet. Let simmer over very low heat for about 2 hours. The mixture should have the consistency of a purée and be a light golden color. Remove the fat, ham, and parsley. Add the peppers to the sauce and let simmer for 15 minutes before straining the sauce through a fine sieve to obtain a light purée. Return the sauce to the skillet. Add the tomato sauce and butter, and season with salt, pepper, and cayenne. Mix thoroughly and let boil for 5 minutes. Set aside.

Peel the remaining 3 cloves garlic and cut them into thin slices. Pour the remaining 1 cup olive oil in a large earthenware casserole or sauté pan. Add the sliced garlic and cook over very low heat. When the garlic slices begin to color, remove them with a slotted spoon. Add the cod pieces, skin side up, and cook for 10 minutes. Remove the fish. Pour out and reserve the olive oil remaining in the casserole. Return the cod to the pan and spoon the sauce over it. Spoon 2 tablespoons of the olive oil evenly over the fish. Return to the heat and warm just to simmering. Serve immediately.

Eggs with Peppers

(Œufs à la piperade)

FOR 6 SERVINGS

3 medium onions
1 pound Espelette or
other mild red or green
bell peppers
2 1/4 pound tomatoes
2 cloves garlic
3 tablespoons olive oil
9 eggs
Salt
Freshly ground pepper
6 thick slices Bayonne ham
(see note)

Cooking time:
35 minutes

Typical of Basque dishes, this recipe calls for simple, fresh ingredients. Fresh eggs, of course, and la piperade: tomatoes, onions and the peppers that give this dish its name, since in the Béarn, piper *means pepper. When you are in Basque country, be sure to buy some of these small sweet peppers — they are delicious.*

Peel and chop the onions. Seed the peppers and cut them into 1-inch-long strips. Peel, seed and quarter the tomatoes. Peel the garlic and cut into thin slices.

Heat the oil in a large skillet over high heat. Add the onions and garlic and sauté for 10 minutes. Add the peppers and cook for 5 minutes. Add the tomatoes, reduce heat and let simmer over medium heat for 15 minutes.

Break the eggs one by one in a large mixing bowl and beat them gently with a fork. Turn the eggs into the skillet over the vegetables. Cook, stirring with a wooden spoon, until the eggs thicken to the consistency of very moist scrambled eggs. Season with salt and pepper and turn the eggs onto a warmed serving plate. Add the ham to the pan and sauté over high heat for 3 seconds on each side. Arrange the ham slices over the eggs and serve immediately.

Note: Bayonne ham is a mildly smoked, salt-cured ham from the Basque region of France. It resembles Parma ham and other prosciuttos. Either of the latter can be substituted, as well as any American cured variety like Smithfield or Virginia country hams.

FOR 6 SERVINGS

6 large squid
(or 12 medium)
5 ounces (3-4 slices)
firm white bread, dried
1/3 cup dry white wine
2 onions
2 cloves garlic
1 bunch flat-leaf parsley
2 thick slices Bayonne ham
(see note)
4 tablespoons olive oil
Salt
Pepper
Pinch cayenne
5 large tomatoes
1 sprig thyme

Special equipment:
Wooden toothpicks

*Cooking time:
About 45 minutes*

These small cousins of the cuttlefish are prepared here with a Basque accent. Often cooked in their ink ("en su tinta"), they are a very famous and pitch-black Spanish Basque specialty. The way I have stuffed them here, however, they are as Marseillais as they are Basque. Note that in France squid go by many names, including chipiron, calamar, encornet, *and, in the Midi,* supion.

Remove the heads from the squid, reserving the tentacles. Gently turn the squid inside out and clean them without piercing the skin. Turn right side out and pat dry.

Remove and discard the crust from the bread and place it in a small bowl with the wine to soak. Peel and chop the onions and garlic. Remove the leaves from the parsley and chop, discarding the stems. Finely chop the ham and the squid tentacles.

Heat 2 tablespoons of the olive oil in a large skillet. Add the onions and garlic and sauté briefly. Add the chopped ham and tentacles. Season with salt and pepper, stir and let cook for 5 minutes.

Remove the bread from the wine and squeeze gently to remove excess liquid. Add the bread to the skillet, breaking it up with the side of a spoon. Remove from the heat and stir in the parsley. Correct the seasoning, and add the cayenne.

Spoon this mixture generously into the squid. Secure the openings closed with two crossed wooden toothpicks. (Or, sew the openings closed with needle and thread.)

Peel the tomatoes and chop them coarsely. Heat the remaining 2 tablespoons olive oil in a large Dutch oven. When the oil is hot, add the stuffed squid and sauté, turning until lightly browned on all sides. Add the tomatoes and the thyme. Cover and let simmer over medium heat for about 30 minutes.

Note: Bayonne ham is a mildly smoked, salt-cured ham from the Basque region of France. It resembles Parma ham and other prosciuttos. Either of the latter can be substituted, as well as any American cured variety like Smithfield or Virginia country hams.

Basque-style Chicken

(Poulet basquaise)

FOR 6 SERVINGS

1 free-range chicken
(about 4 pounds)
1/2 cup olive oil
Salt
Freshly ground pepper
5 cloves garlic
2 pounds fresh Espelette
peppers, or green bell
peppers
4 thick slices Bayonne ham
(about 1/2 pound—see
note)
2 large onions
2 1/4 pounds tomatoes

Cooking time:
50 minutes

This is a chicken fricassee embellished with peppers, tomatoes, onions and, though not everyone adds it, a little Bayonne ham. The generic term Bayonne applies to any salt-cured ham that is air-dried for five months. Oddly, the most famous varieties are not from Bayonne, but from Peyrehorade and Orthez in the Béarn region of France. The following recipe can also be used as a base for Basque-style eggs.

Cut the chicken into 12 pieces. Heat half of the oil in a large Dutch oven. When hot, add the chicken pieces and cook, turning over high heat until lightly browned on all sides. Season with salt and pepper, cover and cook over medium-low heat for 15 minutes.

Peel and chop the garlic. Peel and seed the peppers, and cut them into large pieces. Cut the ham into 1/4 by 1-inch pieces. Add the garlic, peppers, and ham to the pan with the chicken and continue to cook for 20 minutes.

Peel and chop the onions. Peel and seed the tomatoes. Heat the remaining oil in a skillet. Add the onions and cook over medium-low heat for 15 minutes. Add the tomatoes and let cook for 15 minutes longer. Season with salt and pepper and keep warm until ready to serve.

Turn the tomato and onion mixture onto a warmed serving platter. Arrange the chicken pieces, peppers, and ham on top and serve.

Note: Bayonne ham is a mildly smoked, salt-cured ham from the Basque region of France. It resembles Parma ham and other prosciuttos. Either of the latter can be substituted, as well as any American cured variety like Smithfield or Virginia country hams.

108

Béarn-style Stuffed Farm Hen

(Poule au pot béarnaise)

This is a thoroughly regal recipe that has found a place in French history books. I do not know whether school-children are still told about good King Henri, a man who loved ladies and down-to-earth pleasures, but I remember that he was spoken of as a kind ruler so mindful of the plight of his subjects that he worried about what they would eat on Sundays. This noble concern gave birth to poule au pot. Among its many ancient variations, including chickens that have been stuffed, others that have been marinated and cooked in broth, is this authentic and excellent poule au pot béarnaise.

Remove the liver and gizzards from the cavity of the chicken and set them aside. Thoroughly rinse the cavity under cold water and dry with paper towels.

Peel the onion and stick it with the cloves. Peel and chop the garlic and shallot. Remove the leaves from the parsley and tarragon and chop them finely. Mince the ham.

Fill a large Dutch oven or stock pot with 3 quarts water. Add the onion and celery and season with coarse salt and a few peppercorns. Add the chicken liver and gizzards. Bring to a boil, skim off the foam that rises to the top, and let simmer for 30 minutes.

Meanwhile, prepare the stuffing: Remove the crusts from the bread. Place it in a shallow bowl, pour some of the hot broth from the stock pot over it and let soak.

Gently squeeze the bread to remove excess broth and add it to the mixing bowl with the garlic, shallot, parsley, tarragon, chopped ham, egg yolks and pepper. Season with fine salt and mix to blend.

When they have cooked for 30 minutes, remove the liver and gizzards from the stock pot, drain, and chop finely. Add to the stuffing and mix until well blended.

Form the stuffing into loose balls and stuff them into the cavity of the chicken. Sew the opening closed securely and truss the bird. Gently lower the chicken into the simmering broth and let cook over low heat for 1 3/4 hours, skimming off any foam that rises to the surface.

Remove and discard the outer leaves of the cabbage. Plunge it into a saucepan of salted boiling water and blanch for 10 minutes. Rinse under cold water and drain.

FOR 5 TO 6 SERVINGS

1 large, free-range hen (about 4 1/2 pounds), with liver and gizzards
1 onion
2 cloves
1 clove garlic
1 shallot
10 sprigs parsley
2 sprigs tarragon
1/2 pound Bayonne ham (see note)
1 rib celery
Coarse salt
Peppercorns
5 ounces (3-4 slices) firm white bread
2 egg yolks
1 teaspoon freshly ground pepper
Fine salt
1 small savoy cabbage
4 leeks
6 carrots
3 turnips
3 large potatoes

To serve:
Thick slices of country-style bread, toasted
Coarse salt
Freshly ground pepper

Cooking time:
3 hours

Trim and thoroughly rinse the leeks. Rinse and peel the carrots, turnips, and potatoes.

About 45 minutes before the chicken has finished cooking, add the cabbage, leeks, carrots and turnips to the pot. Boil the potatoes separately in a saucepan of salted water for about 30 minutes, or until tender.

To serve, pour the broth into a soup tureen and serve as a first course, ladling it over the toast slices in shallow serving bowls. Cut the chicken into serving-size pieces and arrange on a warmed platter surrounded by the vegetables and the stuffing spooned from the cavity. Accompany with coarse salt and freshly ground pepper.

Note: Bayonne ham is a mildly smoked, salt-cured ham from the Basque region of France. It resembles Parma ham and other prosciuttos. Either of the latter can be substituted, as well as any American cured variety like Smithfield or Virginia country hams.

Gascon Leg of Lamb

(Gigot en gasconnade)

FOR 6 TO 8 SERVINGS

10 cloves garlic
4 onions
2 carrots
2 leeks
1 5-pound leg of lamb
24 anchovy fillets
2 tablespoons olive oil
1 small can tomato paste
(about 4 ounces)
4 tomatoes
3 cups (1 bottle)
hearty red wine,
preferably Madiran
Salt
Pepper

*Cooking time:
1 3/4 hours*

A boast or an exaggeration: this is how the Larousse dictionary defines gasconnade. *But is it really an exaggeration to stud a leg of lamb with anchovies as other cooks do with garlic? Gascons will tell you it is not, and will add that an authentic* gasconnade *is made with mutton, not lamb.*

Peel the garlic cloves. Blanch them in a saucepan of boiling water for 2 minutes. Rinse them under cold water, drain, and pat dry.

Peel and chop the onions and carrots. Trim off and discard the dark green part of the leeks, rinse the leek whites thoroughly under cold water, drain and chop.

Pierce the lamb in several places with the point of a knife and insert the anchovies, distributing them evenly.

Preheat the oven to 350° F.

Heat the olive oil in a large Dutch oven. Add the lamb and sauté quickly on all sides over high heat. Remove from heat. Paint the lamb on all sides with the tomato paste and cook until the lamb is nicely browned.

Add the garlic, onions, carrots, and leeks, and sauté over low heat, stirring until lightly browned. Add the tomatoes and the red wine. Season with salt and pepper. Cover and cook in the preheated oven for 1 1/2 hours.

When cooked, remove and slice the lamb and place it on a warmed serving platter surrounded by the garlic cloves.

Strain the sauce through a fine sieve, correct the seasoning, and pour it over the lamb. Serve with fresh pasta.

113

Toulouse-style Cassoulet

(Cassoulet toulousain)

FOR 10 TO 12 SERVINGS

1 1/4 pounds dried
white beans
1/2 pound slab bacon
3 onions
6 cloves garlic
1 large carrot
2 cloves
15 peppercorns
1 *bouquet garni*
1/2 pound fresh
pork rind
2 quarts cold water
3/4 pound Toulouse-style
sausage
1 uncooked garlic sausage
1 3/4 pounds boned lamb
shoulder
1 pound neck of lamb
3 tablespoons *confit* fat
or bacon fat
Salt
Pepper
2 pounds duck *confit*
(see note)
1 cup fresh breadcrumbs

Cooking time:
5 to 6 hours

According to surveys, cassoulet *is one of the ten favorite dishes of the French. A peasant specialty, its ingredients can vary from one village to the next, but it is always a mixture of beans and meats cooked in an earthenware recipient called a* cassole, *hence its name. Whether it is from Castelnaudary (where it is made mostly with pork), from Carcassonne (containing lamb and partridge in season), or from Toulouse (rounded out with sausage,* confit *and mutton), it is a classic of regional French cooking. Long ago, before white beans were imported from the Americas, it was made with fava beans. Today, purists insist that the only bean to use is the* tarbais, *but other varieties of white beans including* coco *and* lingot *do the trick as well.*

Place the beans in a large bowl. Add enough cold water to cover and let cook for 2 hours. (If using fresh beans, this step is unnecessary.) Blanch the bacon in a saucepan of boiling water for 10 minutes. Rinse under cold water and drain. Cut it into large cubes.

Peel the onions, garlic, and carrot. Stick one of the onions with the 2 cloves. Chop the 2 remaining onions and set aside. Crush the garlic cloves. Slice the carrot into rounds. Tie the peppercorns in a square of cheesecloth.

Drain and rinse the beans.

Place the pork rind in the bottom of a large pan or Dutch oven. Add the beans, bacon, garlic cloves, carrots, *bouquet garni*, the onion stuck with cloves, and the peppercorns. Add the water.

Bring to a boil, skimming off the foam that rises to the surface. Cover and cook over medium-low heat for 1 hour. Add the Toulouse and the garlic sausages. Continue to cook for 30 minutes.

Meanwhile, cut the lamb shoulder and neck into pieces. Heat 2 tablespoons of the *confit* fat in a skillet. Add the lamb, season with salt and pepper and sauté over high heat until browned. Remove and set aside.

Add the chopped onions to the skillet and sauté until wilted. Add about a cup of the liquid in which the beans cooked to the skillet and let simmer for 5 minutes.

Cut the duck *confit* into pieces, brown them quickly in a skillet without any extra fat.

114

Remove the *bouquet garni*, the cheesecloth of peppercorns, and the onion from the Dutch oven, as well as the Toulouse and the garlic sausage. Cut the sausages into 1/2-inch slices.

Preheat the oven to 250° F.

Generously grease a deep ovenproof earthenware casserole with the remaining *confit* fat. Spread a layer of beans over the bottom. Add a layer of meat (bacon, lamb, *confit*, Toulouse and garlic sausage). Add the chopped onions and their juice.

Continue to layer the beans and meat in this manner until all ingredients are used. Sprinkle with 1/2 of the breadcrumbs. Moisten with about 2 cups of the liquid in which the beans cooked.

Sprinkle a little of the melted *confit* or bacon fat over the top. Place in the preheated oven and cook for 4 hours, adding a little additional liquid from the beans as needed, and sprinkling 3 times with the remaining breadcrumbs during the cooking.

Note: Duck *confit* can be purchased in many specialty food stores. Or, make your own following the recipe on page 144.

Basque Cake

(Gâteau basque)

I n his Itineraire nutritif, *a kind of review of France and an anthology of its regional specialties, Grimod de la Reynière neglected to include this Basque cake. It is, nonetheless, a delicious concoction of pastry cream, flour and eggs, one of those earthy, home-style preparations whose light lemony scent perfumes Basque kitchens along the coast near the Spanish border.*

Finely grate the zest from the lemon.

To make the pastry, combine the sugar, salt, lemon zest, whole egg and egg yolk in a mixing bowl. Beat with a whisk until the mixture turns a light lemon yellow. Little by little, incorporate the butter into the mixture. Stir in the flour and work it into the mixture by hand until a dough forms. Roll into a ball and place in the refrigerator to rest for at least 1 hour.

Meanwhile, prepare the pastry cream: Combine the milk and the vanilla bean or vanilla extract in a saucepan and bring to a boil gently. Remove bean.

In a mixing bowl, beat the sugar and egg yolks together with a whisk until the mixture turns a light lemon yellow. Stir in the flour, then the rum. Bit by bit, pour in the hot milk. Pour the mixture back into the saucepan and cook over very low heat, stirring constantly, until it thickens. As soon as it begins to boil, remove from the heat. Float the butter on the surface of the pastry cream and let cool.

Preheat the oven to 400° F.

To assemble the cake, divide the pastry into two unequal parts: two-thirds and one-third. Roll out the larger pastry disk and use it to line the bottom and sides of a buttered 8-inch cake pan. Fill with the cooled pastry cream. Roll out the remaining pastry dough and place on top of the cake, moistening the edges of the top and bottom pastry layers and pressing them firmly together to seal.

Beat the egg and brush it over the top of the cake. Pull the tines of a fork across the top of the pastry several times to make a decorative grid pattern. Prick the pastry with the point of a knife. Place in the preheated oven and cook for 45 minutes. Let cool before unmolding.

FOR 8 SERVINGS

Pastry:
1 lemon, washed and dried
3/4 cup sugar
1/2 teaspoon salt
1 egg
1 egg yolk
10 tablespoons unsalted butter, softened
2 cups flour

Pastry Cream:
1 cup milk
1/2 vanilla bean, broken (or 1 teaspoon vanilla extract)
1/4 cup sugar
2 egg yolks
1/4 cup flour
1 tablespoon rum
1 tablespoon unsalted butter, softened
1 egg

*Cooking time:
About 1 hour*

This county, formed in the nineteenth century, was brought into France's royal realm by King Henri IV. Located in the northeast corner of the Aquitaine, it stretches over the Dordogne, a department much loved by the English.

A magic name on the culinary map of France, the Périgord owes its reputation in large part to its rich natural resources. A country of oak and chestnut trees, the truffle and the chestnut are elbow-to-elbow with the noblest of wild mushrooms, the *cèpe*, and with golden chanterelles. Game is abundant, and crayfish still inhabit the streams of this region.

The Périgord is famous for its *foie gras*, the silky fattened liver of goose and duck; for its stuffed goose neck; for its *confits* lined up in earthenware crocks in the cupboards; and for the fruity walnut oil that gives spirit to its salads. The Périgordins are not overly fond of butter, preferring by far the goose fat that gives a special flavor even to the plainest omelette or sautéed potatoes.

A meal in a country inn of the Périgord is more than worth the detour. If you are lucky, you might taste a soup of vermicelli *gras* (with goose fat). And when you have nearly finished it, you will learn the local custom of *chabrot*—mixing a glass of red Bergerac wine into the last spoonfuls. Or you might  sample a sautéed *foie gras* on a bed of sorrel, a dandelion salad with fresh walnuts, or even *pourpier*, a salad herb that has recently come back into favor.

Your glass will be filled with the dark and hearty wine of Bergerac, unless you prefer the sweet white Monbazillac that our grandmothers enjoyed. The Périgord has everything, from specialties that give France an international reputation to good, simple, everyday fare. The cooking here is naturally flavorful and extremely generous, as if to give back to nature a little of the bounty she has bestowed on this region.

Terrine of Fresh, Fattened Duck Liver

(Terrine de foie gras)

I wish more cooks would prepare their own foie gras, *whether goose or duck, at home. The recipe is simple enough, although (as with anything else) the* foie gras *must be of good quality; otherwise it will melt too much during cooking. Made properly, it is one of the most exquisite feathers in the cap of French gastronomy. Some say that it was invented in Alsace around 1780 by Jean-Pierre Clause, who cooked for Maréchal de Contades, governor of the region. In fact, under Louis XVI,* foie gras pâtés *from Strasbourg were already famous, and a man named Courtois is said to have prepared* foie gras *at least a decade earlier in the city of Périgueux. Today the Périgord's* foie gras *terrine is one of the most famous in the world.*

FOR 4 TO 5 SERVINGS

1 raw fattened duck liver, about 1 pound (see note)
1 teaspoon coarse salt
Pinch freshly ground pepper

Special equipment:
1 terrine slightly smaller than the duck liver

*Cooking time:
1 hour*

Carefully spread apart the lobes of the liver and with the point of a small knife, gently remove the small veins that run through the center.

Season the liver, sprinkling it generously inside and out with the coarse salt and pepper. Press the liver back together and gently fit it into the terrine. Cover with aluminum foil and let marinate, refrigerated, for 2 hours.

Preheat the oven to 195° F.

Place the terrine in a baking pan filled with enough water to come about halfway up the sides of the terrine.

Place in the preheated oven and cook for 1 hour.

Remove from the oven and let rest for 45 minutes. Place a heavy cardboard or wooden template cut to fit the top of the terrine and weigh it down with a heavy object to pack down the liver.

Place in the refrigerator for at least 24 hours before serving.

Remove the liver from the refrigerator 10 minutes before serving.

Cut into 1/2-inch-thick slices and serve with slices of toasted country-style bread.

Note: There is no substitute for the pale silky livers of specially fattened ducks called for in this recipe; ordinary duck livers will not do. There are a few farms in the United States that raise ducks as they do in the Périgord and these farms will ship the raw, vacuum-packed livers.

Garlic Soup

(Tourin)

In the Périgord, the tourin, aromatic with onions and garlic, goose fat and a splash of vinegar, is a very popular dish. It is served steaming hot over souppes, the thin slices of dried-out bread whose name, minus one "p," has been used to describe the dish itself. After all the bread is gone, it is customary to mix a dollop of good red wine into the remaining soup. This is called making the chabrot, or chabrol, and allows the diner to indulge in an extra glassful. This last ingredient is optional, as the soup does very well without it.

Peel and slice the onions. Peel and chop the garlic cloves. Heat the goose fat in a saucepan. Add the onions and cook over low heat until transparent.

Add the chopped garlic and cook for 2 to 3 minutes. Sprinkle the flour over the garlic, stirring with a wooden spoon.

Add the water. Season with salt and pepper and let cook for 15 to 20 minutes.

Place the bread slices in the bottom of a soup tureen. Pour the boiling soup over the bread.

In a small bowl, beat the egg yolks with the vinegar. Add a few tablespoons of the hot soup a little at a time to the egg yolk mixture, stirring constantly.

Stir the egg yolk mixture into the soup tureen. Correct the seasoning, if necessary.

Stir the soup with a ladle and serve immediately.

Note: Goose fat gives this soup its special flavor, but if it is not available, duck or bacon fat can be substituted.

FOR 4 SERVINGS

2 large onions
1 large head garlic
2 tablespoons goose fat (see note)
2 level tablespoons flour
6 cups hot (not boiling) water
Salt
Pepper
Several thin slices dried bread
2 egg yolks
1 tablespoon vinegar

Cooking time:
About 30 minutes

Scrambled Eggs with Truffles

(Œufs brouillés aux truffes)

FOR 4 SERVINGS

7 ounces fresh truffles
(see note)
8 eggs
2 tablespoons *crème fraîche* or heavy cream
Salt
Pepper

*Cooking time:
15 to 20 minutes*

Place a fresh truffle and eggs together in a container with a tight-fitting lid and set aside in a cool spot. The eggs will quickly absorb the aroma of the truffle, thanks to their porous shells. But the truffle's perfume fades a little in this exchange, and the more times you "truffle" eggs, the less flavor you will have in your truffle. The choice is up to you.

The day before, wash, brush, rinse and dry the truffles. Place the truffles and the eggs (in their shells) in a large glass jar or other container with a tight-fitting lid. Close the jar securely and keep cool overnight.

The next day, remove the truffles and slice them thinly.

Break the eggs into a heavy-bottom saucepan. Beat the eggs with a whisk. Add the truffle slices along with any truffle juice. Stir in the cream and season with salt and pepper.

Let rest for 1 hour.

Place the saucepan in a larger saucepan filled with boiling water.

Cook the eggs, stirring constantly over the water bath until the mixture thickens and reaches a creamy consistency. Serve immediately with slices of toasted country-style bread.

Note: If fresh truffles are not available, an equal quantity of canned truffles can be substituted, although the flavor will not be as intense.

Preserved Duck

(Confit de canard)

Conserving and canning food is a way to plan for the future and to make the most of nature's seasonal abundance. At the height of the foie gras season, ducks are plentiful in Périgord markets. The paletots, or the thighs and hindquarters, are most frequently transformed into confits, while the magrets, the meaty breasts, are sold separately for grilling or sautéing. Stored in earthenware crocks protected from the light and in a dry, cool place, confits stay fresh under their layer of rich golden fat for months.

A day in advance, separate the breast halves and the thighs from the carcass, trimming them with a sharp knife.

Remove the fat from under the skin and the carcass, and chop it into 1-inch cubes.

Sprinkle the duck pieces generously on all sides with coarse salt and place them in a large bowl. Cover with a thick layer of the salt and let stand in a cool place for 12 hours.

The next day, remove the meat, rinse and pat dry.

Melt the duck fat over low heat, adding additional fat (rendered duck, goose fat or melted suet) if necessary. (There should be enough fat to cover the pieces completely.) Peel the garlic and add to the pan with the thyme, bay leaf and water.

Add the duck pieces and let them cook at a very slow simmer for about 2 hours. The cooking should be very slow and gentle to keep the meat as tender as possible. Remove the duck pieces from the pan with a slotted spoon. Place them on a wire rack and let them cool quickly. Strain the cooking fat.

When the duck pieces have cooled, place them in an earthenware crock or glass jar. Pour in the strained and cooled fat, covering the duck pieces completely.

Cover the container with plastic wrap and refrigerate.

To serve, remove the duck pieces from the fat and sauté them quickly on all sides in a hot skillet.

Note: The Barbary ducks of France's Southwest are force-fed to produce the precious fat livers used for *foie gras*, and in the process a thick layer of flavorful fat accumulates under their skin. Most ducks not fed in this manner will not have enough fat under the skin to simmer the *confit* properly. You may therefore need to add the rendered fat of another duck or melted suet to have enough fat to cover the duck pieces for simmering and storing.

FOR 4 SERVINGS

2 breast halves (with the skin and fat) of a fattened duck
2 thighs and hind section (with skin and fat) of a fattened duck
Coarse salt
2 to 3 cloves garlic
2 sprigs thyme
1/2 bay leaf
3/4 cup water

Special equipment:
Earthenware crock or large glass jar for storing

Cooking time:
2 hours

Preserved Pork

(Anchaud)

Also spelled enchaux *or* enchaud, *this confit of pork is considered by some to be even more flavorful than the famous goose and duck* confits *of the region. A flat strip of pork, cut from the fillet, is seasoned, rolled, studded with garlic and braised very slowly in fat in a Dutch oven. According to local tradition, the meat has cooked long enough when it can be pierced through with a straw. Like all* confits, anchaud *should be stored in an earthenware crock, completely covered with fat. Serve it cold accompanied by hot vegetables or with a simple salad dressed with walnut oil.*

Two days in advance, bone the pork, or ask your butcher to do it.

Lay it out flat on a work surface, season with salt and pepper.

Crumble the thyme evenly over and roll the meat up to form a roast. Cut in half lengthwise and tie each half securely with string. Roll the two halves in the coarse salt.

Peel the garlic cloves and cut them into 2 or 3 pieces. Stick the garlic into the meat. Refrigerate for 48 hours.

Heat the pork fat in a Dutch oven. Rub the meat with a kitchen towel to remove excess salt.

Place the two pieces of meat in the hot, barely simmering fat.

Let cook at a very low simmer for 2 1/2 hours.

Pierce the meats with a metal skewer to test for doneness. Remove them from the pan and place in an earthenware crock or a glass jar just large enough to hold them.

Strain the fat in which the meat cooked and let cool to lukewarm.

Pour it over the pork to cover completely and to form a seal of fat at least 1 inch deep over the meat.

Store refrigerated for a few weeks before serving. Cut the *anchaud* into thin slices, accompanied by a lamb's-lettuce salad dressed with walnut oil and sautéed potatoes seasoned with garlic.

FOR 6 SERVINGS

3 1/2 pounds pork loin
Fine salt
Freshly ground white pepper
2 sprigs thyme
1/4 to 1/2 cup coarse salt
4 cloves garlic
1 pound pork fat or suet, rendered and clarified

Special equipment:
Earthenware crock or large glass jar for storing

Cooking time:
2 1/2 hours

1 3/4 pounds potatoes
1/3 cup goose fat
(see note)
1 bunch flat-leaf parsley
3 cloves garlic
Salt
Pepper

*Cooking time:
About 15 minutes*

Sarlat-style Potatoes

(Pommes de terre sarladaises)

A mainstay of the region's good home cooking, this is simply potatoes sliced into thin rounds and sautéed in goose fat, with chopped parsley and garlic added at the last moment. Since the town of Sarlat is one of the principle truffle markets of France, some chefs in Paris had the idea of flavoring their potatoes with truffles. But the real pommes Sarladaises have never included them.

Peel the potatoes and cut them into very thin rounds. Rinse, drain thoroughly, and pat dry.

Warm a large cast-iron skillet over high heat until very hot, add the goose fat and let it melt and warm.

Add the potatoes and cook, shaking them from time to time, for about 10 minutes.

Remove the parsley leaves and chop them, discarding the stems.

Peel and finely chop the garlic. Combine the parsley and garlic.

When the potatoes are cooked, season them with salt and pepper.

Sprinkle the parsley and garlic mixture over the potatoes, shaking the pan to distribute the seasoning throughout.

Serve immediately with a *confit.*

Note: Goose fat gives this dish its special flavor, but if it is not available, duck or bacon fat can be substituted.

The garlic can also be added whole and unpeeled to the potatoes at the beginning of the cooking rather than chopped at the last minute. Either way, it flavors the potatoes deliciously.

(Gâteau aux noix)

FOR 8 SERVINGS

Cake:
3 eggs, separated
2 cups sugar
1/2 cup flour
2 tablespoons vanilla sugar
(see note), or 2 tablespoons
sugar and a few
drops vanilla extract
1 tablespoon baking
powder
2/3 cup milk
3 tablespoons *crème
fraîche* or heavy cream
2 tablespoons chopped
walnuts
1 tablespoon unsalted
butter, softened
1 1/2 cups walnut liqueur

Filling:
3 egg yolks
1/2 cup sugar
6 tablespoons flour
1 cup milk
3/4 cup chopped walnuts
2 1/2 tablespoons unsalted
butter, softened

Frosting:
1/2 cup sugar
3/4 cup water
2 ounces semisweet
chocolate, chopped
4 tablespoons unsalted
butter, softened

Special equipment:
1 8-cup charlotte mold

*Cooking time:
About 1 hour*

The Périgord and the Dauphiné regions have most of France's walnut groves, as well as a walnut museum in Doissat, not far from Europe's largest walnut forest. So this cake has a particularly strong following here.

Preheat the oven to 500° F.

To make the cake dough, place the egg yolks in a large mixing bowl with the sugar. Beat until the mixture is frothy and a pale lemon yellow. Add the flour and mix thoroughly. Stir in the vanilla sugar and baking powder. Add the milk a little at a time, stirring. Stir in the *crème fraîche*, beating until the mixture is thick and forms a ribbon. Stir in the chopped nuts.

In a separate mixing bowl, beat the egg whites until firm peaks form. Fold them gently into the egg-yolk mixture.

Coat the charlotte mold with the butter. Pour in the batter.

Place in the center of the preheated oven and cook for 5 to 7 minutes. Reduce to 400° F. and cook for 35 minutes longer, or until the cake springs back when pressed gently in the center.

Remove from the oven and let cool in the charlotte mold.

Meanwhile, prepare the filling: Combine the egg yolks and sugar and beat until pale lemon yellow. Stir in the flour.

In a small saucepan, heat the milk gently until simmering. Pour a small amount of the hot milk into the egg-yolk mixture, stirring, then gradually stir in the remaining hot milk. Turn the mixture back into the saucepan and warm over medium-low heat, stirring constantly, until it thickens. Remove from the heat and mix in the walnuts and butter. Let cool to lukewarm.

Turn the cake out of the charlotte mold and carefully cut horizontally into three slices. Place the walnut liqueur in a large shallow bowl and dip the cut sides of the cake slices into it.

Place the bottom cake slice on a plate and spread half of the cooled filling mixture over the top. Cover with the second slice and the remaining filling. Top with the third slice.

To make the frosting, combine the sugar and water in a small saucepan. Place over medium heat and cook until it thick and syrupy. Remove from the heat, add the chocolate, cover and let stand for 5 minutes. Stir in the butter.

While still warm, spread the frosting over the cake.

Note: To make vanilla sugar, bury a vanilla bean in a large glass jar filled with a pound of sugar, close the jar tightly and let sit for a week or two.

BRETAGNE NORMANDIE

One day, a caprice of the Couesnon river formed the Mont Saint-Michel in Normandy, creating an almost immutable border between two regions fiercely attached to their differences.

On one side is Brittany, both rugged and mild, with its black forests, its peat bogs and golden juniper bushes, its indescribable light and its howling winds, and its arched and jagged coastline.

On the other side is Normandy, tart as a green apple, but creamy as well, picturesque as a postcard, sweet and rich.

These are flat regions graced with an occasional ripple, regions in which the sea is never far but whose deepest inland zones seem untouched by sea air.

There are ten districts in all, from the Seine-Maritime to the Loire Atlantique, and their cooking is characterized by dishes that have changed as little as possible from their natural state.

In fact, in Brittany, they will tell you that gastronomy does not exist. It is only here, Bretons will say, that foods retain their true flavor. To me, Brittany's cuisine is a precise illustration of what I said in the preface of this book about the quality of ingredients. Here are the best lobsters and oysters, sometimes the best abalone, delicious lightly salted butter, fresh-caught fish, lively crustaceans and shellfish, pampered pigs, oats for porridges and buckwheat for crêpes. Brittany also grows the mini-vegetables that are so much in style right now, eggplant and zucchini like those found in the heart of the Midi and on Belle-Île, and

melons as sweet as those of Cavaillon. There are no olive groves here yet, but there are superb colza fields.

In short, there is no lack of good products in Brittany. And even if the Bretons occasionally cook their fish too long, it might be better not to tell them so.

As for Normandy, the best is never confused with the merely good, and the Normand *cuisine* is overwhelmingly generous.

Cream flows freely and it sometimes seems to have a faint scent of Calvados. The veal is carefully bred and lovingly prepared. Ducks are prepared *au sang*, in their blood, or *à la rouennaise*, and the Camembert, Livarot and Pont-L'Évêque are some of France's most prized cheeses.

And then there are the ciders and Calvados, golden liquids the color of candied apples. The first, the region's most popular beverage, is also widespread in Brittany, though to a lesser extent since there are also wines in the area around Nantes.

The second, Calvados, reaches its apogee in Normandy's Auge Valley, where the heady perfume of dried apples, from the bottles in the cellars to apples drying in attics, is unequalled anywhere else on earth.

Buckwheat Crêpes

(Crêpes de blé noir)

I do not know if there are Breton households in which crêpes are still made on a black cast-iron billig *that has been generously greased with suet. Today, we are more likely to go to a crêperie. Too, fifty years ago, appetites were heartier. Ten crêpes at a sitting daunted no one, and bets were won and lost on who could eat the most.*

The taste of buckwheat crêpes is inimitable: crisp and light, with a little salted butter melting in the center. I can do without the fillings—ham, egg, sausage or andouille *—even if* la crêpe garnie *is currently in fashion. I have nothing against them, but please spare us crêpes filled with* merguez *sausage or* ratatouille, *which do, unfortunately, exist.*

FOR 30 CRÊPES

1 1/2 cups buckwheat flour
1/3 cup all-purpose flour
1 egg
Pinch salt
4 tablespoons butter, melted
2 cups water
1/4 cup beer or water

Cooking time:
About 45 minutes

Combine the buckwheat and all-purpose flour in a large mixing bowl. Add the egg and salt and work them into the flour.

Add 2 tablespoons of the melted butter a little at a time, mixing. Slowly pour in the water.

Beat the mixture vigorously; the batter should have the consistency of light cream. Let rest for 2 to 3 hours, refrigerated.

Just before making the crêpes, stir the 1/4 cup beer or water into the batter to lighten it.

Heat a large crêpe pan over medium-high heat and wipe the surface with a cloth or paper towel dipped in the remaining melted butter. Pour a small ladleful of the batter into the center of the hot pan, turning it quickly with a circular motion to spread it evenly over the surface.

Cook until lightly browned, then turn the crêpe with a spatula or flip it gently and cook until lightly browned on the other side.

Turn it onto a warm plate and keep warm while preparing the remaining crêpes.

Serve immediately, filled with grated cheese, eggs, bacon, or simply with a little salted butter.

136

Mussels with White Wine and Shallots

(Moules à la marinière)

FOR 6 SERVINGS

5 to 6 pounds mussels, preferably the small *bouchots*
4 shallots
6 sprigs parsley
10 tablespoons butter
3/4 cup dry white wine
Freshly ground pepper
1 sprig thyme
Salt

*Cooking time:
10 minutes*

*T*his is the simplest way to prepare mussels, and a perfect occasion to gather plenty of friends around the table for a huge steaming stock pot fragrant with white wine and shallots.

The mussel, an inexpensive mollusk, is prepared in many different ways in France, depending on the region. The most spectacular is certainly l'éclade, *a recipe from Charente-Maritime. For this, the mussels are arranged on a bed of dry pine needles and set ablaze. After a minute or two they are cooked and ready to be eaten sizzling hot.*

Wash the mussels, scraping to remove their grassy "beards."

Peel and chop the shallots. Remove the parsley leaves and chop them finely. Melt 3 tablespoons of the butter in a large heavy skillet or saucepan.

Add the shallots and cook until wilted.

Add the wine, a sprinkling of pepper, and thyme. Let simmer for 5 minutes. Add the mussels, cover and cook over high heat, shaking the pan often so that all the mussels open at about the same time. Take off the cover, remove the mussels as they open, and place them on a warmed serving platter.

When all the mussels have opened, empty the pan, and strain the cooking broth through a fine sieve. Wipe out the pan and return the broth to it. Cook briefly over high heat until boiling.

Cut the remaining butter into small pieces. Remove the saucepan from the heat and whisk the butter into the broth a little at a time.

Correct the seasoning, if necessary.

Pour the sauce over the mussels, sprinkle with the chopped parsley, and serve.

Brittany-style Scallops

(Coquilles Saint-Jacques à la bretonne)

FOR 4 SERVINGS

12 large sea scallops
Salt
Freshly ground pepper
8 small new potatoes
10 sprigs parsley
2 tablespoons flour
7 tablespoons unsalted butter
Juice of 1 lemon
1 tablespoon *crème fraîche* or heavy cream

Special equipment: Steamer

Cooking time: 5 minutes

In France, the fishing of bivalves is regulated by law, so after about the end of May you can be sure that the scallops served in restaurants are not from French waters. Once abundant in Northern Spain, scallops were the badge of religious sojourners who reached the Spanish pilgrimage site of Saint Jacques de Compostelle: the scallop shell around their necks indicated that they had completed the journey.

I remember a dish frequently served in Brittany on holidays: the scallops from two shells were used to stuff three, thanks to the addition of chopped onions, parsley, and breadcrumbs. This dish was eaten at lunch, in the evening and, occasionally, the next day as well. And we would willingly have eaten them for yet another meal. In the following recipe the scallops are prepared simply à la meunière, *sliced in half, sautéed in butter and accompanied by steamed potatoes.*

Ask your fishmonger to prepare the scallops, reserving the roe, if possible. Slice the scallops in half horizontally. Spread them on a paper towel to dry. Season with salt and pepper.

Peel and rinse the potatoes. Cook them in a steamer until tender.

Remove the leaves from the parsley and chop, discarding the stems.

Place the flour in a shallow bowl and roll the scallops in it, shaking off excess flour.

Heat 5 tablespoons of the butter in a large skillet. Add the scallops (and their roe, if using) and cook over high heat, about 2 minutes on each side, sprinkling them with the lemon juice halfway through the cooking. Sprinkle with the parsley, remove from the skillet, arrange on a serving platter, and keep warm while preparing the sauce.

Melt the remaining butter in the skillet, and heat until the foam subsides, scraping the pan with a wooden spoon to loosen the flavorful bits that stick to the bottom. Stir in the *crème fraîche* and remove from the heat. Pour the sauce over the scallops and surround with the steamed potatoes.

The scallops can also be served in their shells, with the potatoes on the side.

140

Stuffed Clams

(Palourdes farcies)

Every region has its own specialty of farcis, and Brittany is no exception. The shellfish lover may think it is gilding the lily to stuff clams with garlic and parsley to highlight their delicious almond-like flavor. But this recipe can also be used for some of the less noble mollusks like the grosses berniques of the barnacle family, or vernis, venus shells, which are considerably improved by this combination.

Wash the clams thoroughly in several changes of cold water to remove the sand.

Place them in a large saucepan or stock pot with a little salted water. Cover and cook over high heat, shaking the pan from time to time.

Remove the clams one by one as they open. Remove and discard the top shell of each clam.

Peel the garlic cloves. Remove the leaves from the parsley, discarding the stems. Finely chop the garlic and parsley together and place them in a mixing bowl.

Add the softened butter and breadcrumbs to the mixing bowl and stir until well combined. Season with salt and pepper.

Stuff some of the seasoned butter around each clam in its half shell.

Arrange the clams on a large baking pan lined with a layer of coarse salt (to keep the shells from tipping), or arrange them on heatproof plates with round indents to hold the shells.

Place under a hot broiler for 2 to 3 minutes.

Serve immediately with slices of country bread.

FOR 4 SERVINGS

4 dozen clams, such as cherrystones
Salt
6 cloves garlic
1 bunch parsley
10 tablespoons butter, softened
1/4 cup breadcrumbs
Freshly ground pepper
Coarse salt

Cooking time:
10 minutes

1 3/4 pound boneless
pork loin
1/2 pound pork liver
1/2 pound fatty slab bacon
1 shallot
1 clove garlic
4 teaspoons salt
1 teaspoon freshly ground
pepper
Pinch allspice
3 eggs
1 tablespoon cognac
1 large thin sheet barding
fat or several strips thinly
sliced bacon

Cooking time:
1 1/2 hours

Country Pâté

(Pâté de campagne)

*F*rance loves *pâtés. Classic versions, which have evolved from recipes that originated in the Middle Ages, are always presented in a pastry dough, or* en croûte. *At one time* pâtés *were nearly ubiquitous. In a meal served to Monseigneur d'Estampes by the fourteenth-century chef Taillevent, for example, there were no less than three: one made of capon, another of venison and a third of pears, in the form of what we would today call a* tourte. *The* grande cuisine *of the nineteenth century gave us complicated, architectural elaborations, but the provinces contributed the lion's share, sending the best examples of their regional art to the capital: from Rouen came* veau de rivière, *made with Normandy calf raised in the meadows bordering the Seine; from Pithiviers, wild lark* pâté; *and Perigueux distinguished itself with its terrine of partridge and truffles. My Brittany country* pâté *may seem simple beside these culinary marvels, but that is part of its appeal.*

Preheat the oven to 350° F.

Chop the pork loin, liver, and bacon separately (or ask your butcher to grind them separately), and place them in a large mixing bowl.

Peel and finely chop the shallot and garlic. Add them to the meat. Season with the salt, pepper, and allspice. Work the ingredients together.

Add the eggs and cognac and mix thoroughly.

Use 3/4 of the fat or strips of bacon to line the bottom and sides of an earthenware *pâté* terrine large enough to hold the mixture.

Fill the lined terrine with the meat, distributing it evenly.

Cover with the remaining piece of fat or bacon strips. Cover tightly with a lid or with a piece of heavy-duty foil.

Place in the preheated oven and cook for 1 1/2 hours.

To check for doneness, insert the point of a sharp knife into the center of the *pâté*; it should pull out easily without any trace of red juices.

Remove from the oven and let cool completely before serving.

143

Mackerel in White Wine

(Maquereaux au vin blanc)

*T*hose who trawl fish in Brittany frequently pull in more mackerel than they can use; so many, in fact, that you might think they were the only fish in the sea. I have memories of an exquisite maquereau à la moutarde, *as well as* filets de maquereaux au vin blanc, *served early in the morning and doused with a glass of Muscadet wine, a kind of Breton* mâchon.

Note: Always choose small mackerel such as those called lisette *from the Dieppe coast. They are the best.*

Trim, gut and rinse the mackerel, or ask your fishmonger to do it for you.

Peel the carrots and onions, and slice them into very thin rounds. Slice the lemon into thin rounds.

Spread half of the carrot, onion, and lemon slices over the bottom of a deep ovenproof casserole or Dutch oven large enough to hold the fish. Arrange the mackerel on top, side by side and head to tail.

Cover with the remaining sliced vegetables and lemon rounds.

Sprinkle with the peppercorns and salt. Add the thyme, bay leaf and clove.

Add the wine and place the pan over low heat. Bring to a boil, reduce heat and let simmer for 1 minute.

Carefully remove the fish and place them in a large terrine.

Place the liquid and seasoning in the pan over high heat and let boil for 5 minutes. Pour this reduced liquid over the mackerel in the terrine.

Let cool to room temperature. Refrigerate for at least 1 hour.

Serve with toasted bread and salted butter.

FOR 6 SERVINGS

24 small mackerel
2 carrots
2 medium onions
1 lemon, washed and dried
Black peppercorns
Salt
3 sprigs thyme
1/2 bay leaf
1 clove
3 cups (1 bottle) dry white wine, preferably Muscadet

Cooking time:
About 6 minutes

2 1/4 pounds skate,
preferably thornback
1 quart water
1/2 cup vinegar
Salt
1 tablespoon strong
mustard
2 tablespoons capers
7 tablespoons unsalted
butter
Freshly ground pepper

Special equipment:
Ovenproof earthenware
platter

*Cooking time:
10 minutes*

Skate with Brown Butter Sauce

(Raie au beurre noisette)

This recipe calls for brown butter, since black butter is now considered toxic because of the acrolein released when it is cooked at high temperatures.

Nevertheless, black butter has featured in recipes since the sixteenth century, when butter first made its appearance in French cooking. Before that, oil, lard or suet served the purpose. Skate comes from Northern waters and the English Channel, and the most commonly found and desirable variety is the bouclée, *or thornback. Its lean, delicately ridged flesh is particularly good in the winter. Do not worry about buying skate that has a very faint odor of ammonia, since this is an indication of freshness.*

Rinse and scrub the skate thoroughly under cold running water.

Place in a large baking pan of boiling water and blanch for 1 minute. Drain.

Lay the skate on a work surface and peel off the skin (or ask your fishmonger to do this). Cut the fish into 4 pieces.

Place the pieces in a large, deep-sided sauté pan or skillet with the water, vinegar, and a little salt. Simmer gently over low heat, without boiling, for about 5 minutes.

Drain the fish thoroughly, and brush a little of the mustard over each piece. Place on the preheated earthenware platter. Crush the capers with a fork and sprinkle them evenly over the fish.

Melt the butter in a small skillet. Season with salt and pepper and cook until it begins to sizzle and turns a light brown.

Remove from the heat and pour immediately over the fish.

Serve very hot, accompanied by steamed potatoes.

Sole in Butter Sauce

(Sole meunière)

Normandy has beautiful sole, especially the tiny céteaux that are caught around the islands of Oléron and Ré. One of the royal dishes served to Louis XIV, sole is considered the noblest of fish. The most expensive variety is without doubt the sole de ligne. The great chefs of the nineteenth century competed with each other to come up with the most ingenious preparation of this fish, but the simplest method of preparing it is à la meunière, floured lightly, sautéed quickly, then drizzled with foaming butter and a splash of lemon juice.

Carefully pat the sole dry. Remove the leaves from the parsley and chop, discarding the stems.

Season the sole with salt and pepper.

Spread the flour over a large plate and dredge each sole in it briefly, gently shaking off the excess flour.

Melt about 4 tablespoons of the butter with the oil in a very large skillet (or two skillets). When the butter is hot, add as many of the sole as the pan will hold comfortably, skin side down, and cook over high heat for 5 minutes. Carefully turn the fish with a large spatula and cook 5 minutes longer. Repeat for remaining sole.

Transfer the fish to a warmed serving platter. Sprinkle with the lemon juice and chopped parsley.

Melt the remaining butter in the skillet. When it turns a light brown, remove from the heat and pour over the sole. The hot butter will foam on contact with the parsley and lemon juice.

Serve immediately.

FOR 6 SERVINGS

6 individual-size sole, black skin removed
12 sprigs parsley
Salt
Freshly ground pepper
6 tablespoons flour
14 tablespoons salted butter
2 tablespoons vegetable oil
Juice of 1 lemon

Cooking time:
10 minutes

Lobster with Herb Butter

(Homard au beurre d'herbes)

A n absolutely delectable crustacean, this "cardinal of the seas" has a midnight-blue shell flecked with green that turns brilliant scarlet when cooked.

The recipes of la grand cuisine classique *do not always do it justice; in fact, they often overpower it. Lobster should be prepared simply, as it is here, to keep its incomparable flavor intact.*

Plunge the heads of the lobster into a large stock pot of boiling water and cook for 2 minutes. Cut the butter into pieces and let soften slightly.

Remove the leaves from the parsley, chervil, and tarragon, and chop them finely, discarding the stems. Combine these herbs, the chopped chives and coarse salt in a food processor and process. Add the butter and process to make a soft spread. Add the lemon juice and mix. Season with pepper and add more salt, if necessary, and process once more.

Preheat the oven to 450° F.

Cut the lobsters in half lengthwise and remove the black portion. Spread some of the herb butter over each lobster half.

Arrange them cut side up in a large baking pan. Place in the preheated oven and cook for 10 to 12 minutes.

Serve immediately.

FOR 4 SERVINGS

4 lobsters, about 1 pound each
1/2 cup unsalted butter
10 sprigs parsley
10 sprigs chervil
4 sprigs tarragon
1 tablespoon chives
1 tablespoon coarse salt
Juice of 1/2 lemon
Freshly ground pepper

Cooking time:
About 15 minutes

(Canette
aux navets)

FOR 4 SERVINGS

1 duckling (about
4 1/2 pounds)
Salt
Freshly ground pepper
1 carrot
1 shallot
1 leek
5 tablespoons butter
3 tablespoons oil
1 *bouquet garni*
1 2/3 cups water
2 1/4 pounds small,
new turnips
12 small new onions
1/2 teaspoon chives

Cooking time:
Bouillon, 35 minutes
Duckling, 40 minutes

For this recipe, I use a Challans duckling from the Vendée area and a lot of tender new turnips. Whether they are from Belle-Île or from Nantes, these turnips are famous and among the best accompaniments for duck, since they absorb its delicious juices as they cook.

Rinse, pat dry, and truss the duckling, reserving the liver, gizzards, wing tips and neck to make a bouillon. Season the duckling on all sides with salt and pepper.

Peel and chop the carrot and shallot. Discard all but the white part of the leek, rinse thoroughly, and cut into rounds.

Melt 1 tablespoon of the butter with 1 tablespoon of the oil in a saucepan, add the liver, gizzards, wing tips, and neck and sauté quickly. Add the chopped carrot, shallot, and leek, the *bouquet garni* and water. Let simmer over medium heat for 30 minutes.

Strain the bouillon in which the duck parts and vegetables cooked through a fine sieve, pressing with the back of a spoon to extract all of the juices.

Melt the remaining butter and oil together in a large Dutch oven.

Add the duckling and sauté quickly until lightly browned on all sides. Remove the duckling and pour off the fat in the pan. Return the duckling to the pan, along with the strained bouillon. Place over low heat and cook, partly covered, for 30 minutes.

Peel the turnips and onions. Bring a saucepan of salted water to a boil. Blanch the turnips and onions separately in the boiling water for 1 minute. Drain and pat dry.

Add the turnips and onions to the pan with the duck and let cook 20 minutes longer. Correct the seasoning.

Remove the duck and cut it into serving-size pieces. Arrange on a warmed serving platter surrounded by the turnips and onions.

Pour the pan juices over the duck and sprinkle with the chopped chives.

153

Auge Valley Chicken

(Poulet vallée d'Auge)

Normandy is apple and cider country and, consequently, it is the land of Calvados, France's famous apple brandy. For this Vallée d'Auge chicken you will need a little crème fraîche *and a generous dose of this amber liquid that perfumes the air with the scent of apples from at least ten feet away. This is a very fitting combination, since the only Calvados meriting an* appellation controlée *classification is distilled in the Auge Valley.*

Cut the chicken into 8 pieces, or ask your butcher to do it. Season with salt and pepper.

Trim off the stem ends of the mushrooms, rinse the mushrooms briefly under cold water, dry with a kitchen towel and chop. Peel and chop the shallot.

Melt the butter in a large, deep-sided skillet. Add the chicken pieces. Crumble the thyme leaves and bay leaf between the fingers and sprinkle over the chicken.

Cook over low heat, without letting the chicken brown, for 15 minutes. When the pieces have turned white on all sides, add the mushrooms and shallot. Cook for several minutes longer.

Sprinkle with the Calvados and ignite, being careful to avert your face from the flames. Gently lift the chicken pieces with a wooden spoon to help distribute the Calvados evenly.

Add the cream and stir gently. Correct the seasoning, if necessary.

Cover and continue to cook for 18 minutes.

When cooked, arrange the chicken pieces and mushrooms in a warm, deep serving platter.

Let the sauce in the pan reduce slightly and pour it over the chicken.

Serve with *pommes en l'air:* apples that have been peeled, sliced and sautéed in a skillet.

FOR 4 TO 5 SERVINGS

1 large farm chicken
(about 3 1/2 pounds)
Salt
Freshly ground pepper
1/2 pound cultivated
mushrooms
1 shallot
3 1/2 tablespoons unsalted
butter
1 sprig thyme
1/2 small bay leaf
5 tablespoons Calvados
1 cup *crème fraîche*
or heavy cream

Cooking time:
About 40 minutes

3 tablespoons oil
1 1-inch-thick center cut
slice of raw ham with bone
(about 3 1/2 pounds)
Salt
Freshly ground pepper
3 sprigs thyme
12 cloves garlic
1/4 cup water
8 large potatoes
4 sprigs flat-leaf parsley

Cooking time:
About 1 3/4 hours

Grilled "Wheel" of Fresh Pork with Potatoes

(Rouelle de porc aux pommes de terre)

A piece cut from the center of the leg, the rouelle resembles a wheel, surrounded by a handsome layer of fat and a sturdy rind that gets crisp during the cooking. This flavorful piece of pork is too often overlooked. Served with tender, thick-cut potato fries that cook in the pan with the meat, it is one of the most satisfying examples of traditional, home-style cooking.

Preheat the oven to 350° F.

Heat the oil in a large ovenproof roasting pan.

Add the ham slice and sauté on both sides until lightly browned.

Season with salt and pepper. Crumble the thyme leaves evenly over all.

Arrange the garlic cloves (unpeeled) around the meat. Add the water and place in the preheated oven to cook for 45 minutes, basting occasionally.

Meanwhile, peel, rinse, and dry the potatoes. Cut them lengthwise in the shape of thick French fries.

Remove the leaves from the parsley and chop, discarding the stems.

Turn the meat and baste with a little more hot water, if necessary. Arrange potatoes around the meat and return to the oven to cook for 45 minutes longer.

When the meat has finished cooking, transfer it to a warmed serving platter. Arrange the potatoes and garlic cloves around it. Salt the potatoes, if necessary.

Add a little hot water to the roasting pan and place over medium heat, scraping the pan with a wooden spoon to loosen the flavorful bits that stick to the bottom. Pour the pan juices over the meat. Sprinkle with the parsley and serve.

Veal Roast with Mushrooms

(Rognonnade de veau)

The traditional cut used for this preparation is taken from the loin with part of the kidney still attached. This was how the loin was sold in the French provinces thirty or forty years ago. Today it usually has to be ordered, since the kidneys are now sold separately. Needless to say, it is a choice cut of meat.

Not so long ago, the only good French veal came from calves raised in Normandy along the banks of the Seine, and that is why I have included the rognonnade *in this chapter.*

Lard the roast and tie it securely with kitchen string, or ask your butcher to prepare it. Season with salt and pepper.

Peel the onions and carrots. Chop the onions, and cut the carrots into 1 by 1/4 by 1/4-inch pieces. Cut the bacon into small cubes, first removing any rind.

Melt the oil and 2 tablespoons of the butter together in a Dutch oven large enough to hold the roast. Add the onions, carrots, and bacon and sauté gently. Remove them with a slotted spoon, leaving no bits of vegetable or bacon in the pan.

Add the roast to the pan and brown lightly on all sides over medium heat. Remove it from the pan.

Return the onions, carrots and bacon to the pan. Crumble the thyme leaves over the vegetables and lay the roast on top.

Add 1/2 cup of the bouillon. Cover the pan and let cook over low heat for 1 3/4 hours, adding the remaining bouillon as needed during the cooking and turning the roast from time to time.

If the pan juices seem a little thin, leave the cover of the pan ajar slightly to allow them to reduce.

While the meat cooks, trim, rinse, and dry the mushrooms. Cut them into quarters.

Melt the 3 remaining tablespoons butter in a large saucepan.

Add the mushrooms and lemon juice. Season with salt and pepper.

Cover and let cook over high heat for 20 minutes.

Remove the roast from the pan, remove the string, slice and place on a warmed serving platter. Arrange the mushrooms around the veal.

Strain the juices from the roasting pan through a fine sieve.

Correct the seasoning, pour into a sauceboat and pass with the veal.

FOR 8 SERVINGS

1 veal roast
(about 4 pounds)
Salt
Freshly ground pepper
5 medium onions
2 carrots
1/4 pound slab bacon
5 tablespoons butter
1 tablespoon oil
1 sprig thyme
1 cup veal or beef bouillon
1 pound cultivated mushrooms
Juice of 1 lemon

Cooking time:
Veal, about 2 hours
Mushrooms, 20 minutes

4 large prime veal chops,
cut 1-inch thick
Salt
Freshly ground pepper
20 small new white onions
3/4 pound cultivated
mushrooms
2 tablespoons unsalted
butter
2 tablespoons Calvados
3/4 cup *crème fraîche*
or heavy cream

*Cooking time:
35 minutes*

Normandy-style Veal Chops

(Côte de veau normande)

The perfect veal chop is a slowly cooked, thick cut of meat. And of course, à la normande means the dish features lots of good butter and cream, both of which are plentiful in Normandy.

Peel the onions. Blanch them in a saucepan of boiling salted water for 2 minutes. Drain and pat dry.

Trim the stem ends from the mushrooms. Rinse and dry them, and cut into quarters.

Season the veal chops on both sides with salt and pepper.

Melt the butter in a large skillet. Add the veal chops and brown over high heat on both sides. Reduce the heat to medium, add the onions and let cook for 10 minutes.

Add the mushrooms, and cook for 10 minutes longer.

Transfer the veal chops, onions, and mushrooms to a warmed serving platter.

Add the Calvados to the skillet. Warm gently and ignite, being careful to avert your face from the flames.

Stir in the cream, stirring and scraping the pan with a wooden spoon to loosen the flavorful bits that stick to the bottom. Correct the seasoning, if necessary. Let the sauce boil briefly before pouring it over the veal. Serve immediately.

Veal Stew

(Blanquette de veau)

Blanquette, *from* blanc, *the French word for white, is a preparation of simmered veal which can include a white roux, as well as cream and eggs. Blanquette de veau is a classic of French culinary heritage. Not typically from any one region, it fits in well in Normandy, land of cream, eggs, and butter.*

Cut the veal into 2-inch pieces. Peel the carrots and onion. Cut the carrots into thin rounds. Stick the onion with a clove. Tie the celery, parsley, thyme, and bay leaf together in a *bouquet garni.*

Melt 3 1/2 tablespoons of the butter with the oil in a Dutch oven. Add the veal in small batches and brown on all sides, removing each batch when browned. Return all of the veal to the pan. Add the carrots, onion, *bouquet garni*, coarse salt and a few peppercorns.

Add the water, which should cover the meat by about 1/2 inch. (Add more water if necessary to cover.)

Place over high heat and bring to a boil. Reduce the heat, cover and let simmer for 45 minutes.

Meanwhile, peel the pearl onions. Trim the stem ends from the mushrooms, rinse, dry and cut them into quarters. Melt 3 tablespoons of the remaining butter in a skillet. Add the mushrooms, season with salt and pepper, and sauté until lightly browned. Remove the mushrooms from the pan. Melt the remaining 2 1/2 tablespoons of butter in the skillet, add the onions and sauté briefly. Return the mushrooms to the skillet and keep warm while finishing the sauce.

FOR 6 SERVINGS

1 3/4 pounds veal breast
1 1/2 pounds veal flank
2 carrots
1 onion
1 clove
1 rib celery
3 sprigs parsley
2 sprigs thyme
1 bay leaf
9 tablespoons unsalted butter
1 tablespoon oil
1 tablespoon coarse salt
Peppercorns
1 quart Evian or other bottled water
18 pearl onions
1/2 pound cultivated mushrooms
Fine salt
Freshly ground pepper

For the Sauce:
2 egg yolks
1/2 cup *crème fraîche* or heavy cream
Juice of 1 lemon
Salt
Freshly ground pepper

Cooking time:
1 hour

160

Place the egg yolks in a large bowl and combine with the cream and half of the lemon juice. Season with salt and pepper. Stir a little of the cooking liquid from the meat into the sauce.

Remove the meat from the pan and place it on a warmed shallow serving bowl with the mushrooms and onions. Remove the *bouquet garni*, the carrots and onion from the bouillon.

Pour the egg yolk-cream mixture into the bouillon, whisking. Place the pan over very low heat, whisking constantly, being very careful not to let the sauce boil. Correct the seasoning, adding the remaining lemon juice if necessary.

Pour the sauce over the meat and serve immediately with rice.

Note: The meat for the *blanquette* may be prepared in advance, but the sauce should be made at the last minute since it can not be reheated.

Cauliflower Gratin

(Gratin de chou-fleur)

FOR 6 SERVINGS

1 large head cauliflower
Salt
5 tablespoons unsalted butter
2 1/2 tablespoons flour
2 cups milk
Grated nutmeg
Freshly ground pepper
3/4 cup grated Gruyère cheese
1/2 cup grated Parmesan cheese
2 tablespoons *crème fraîche* or heavy cream
1 egg yolk
2 tablespoons fresh breadcrumbs (see note)

Cooking time: 30 minutes

In the vast range of gratins, there are those that figure in French grande cuisine because of their use of such so-called noble products as sole, lobster, and scallops. And then there are everyday gratins, sprinkled with breadcrumbs or grated Gruyère cheese and baked in the oven until the top is golden brown. In a Brittany rich with cauliflower, this is a traditional family recipe, and a dish that can be prepared in advance and placed in the oven at the last moment.

Cut the base and green leaves from the cauliflower. Remove any browned or damaged flowerets. Cut out the core.

Place about 1 inch of salted water in a saucepan large enough to hold the cauliflower. Bring to a boil, add the cauliflower, stem side down. Return to a boil, cover the pan and let cook for 15 minutes.

Meanwhile, prepare the sauce: Melt 2 tablespoons of the butter in a heavy-bottom saucepan. Stir in the flour and cook briefly.

Heat the milk in a separate saucepan and add it to the flour-butter mixture, whisking constantly. Season with nutmeg, salt and pepper, and simmer for 10 minutes.

Stir in 1/2 cup of the Gruyère and 1/3 cup of the Parmesan, the *crème fraîche*, and egg yolk. Mix thoroughly.

Preheat the oven to 475° F.

In a small bowl, combine the remaining Gruyère and Parmesan with the breadcrumbs.

Drain the cauliflower and separate into flowerets, and place them in a buttered *gratin* dish. Pour the sauce over and sprinkle the cheese-breadcrumb mixture evenly over the top. Cut the remaining butter into small pieces and distribute evenly over the breadcrumbs.

Place in the preheated oven and cook for 10 minutes.

Note: To make fresh breadcrumbs, remove and discard the crusts from 1 or 2 slices of white bread. Place the bread in a blender or food processor and process briefly with an on-off motion until reduced to soft crumbs.

Pastry-Wrapped Pears

(Douillons)

A good cook gives his imagination free rein when it comes to desserts. A douillon *is a pear wrapped in bread dough or pie pastry, a variation on another Norman specialty called* bourdelot *that uses an apple instead. A kind of golden turnover, it can*  contain, if the cook chooses, a delicious whiff of Calvados.

FOR 4 SERVINGS

1 pound bread dough
4 large pears, ripe but firm
5 1/2 tablespoons unsalted butter
1 egg yolk, lightly beaten
3/4 cup *crème fraîche* or
1 cup heavy cream, whipped
Vanilla sugar (see note)

Cooking time:
30 minutes

If using frozen bread, thaw the bread dough according to package directions.

Rinse the pears and pat them dry, being careful not to break off the stems.

Let the butter soften slightly, then cut it into small pieces and work it into the bread dough, kneading the dough for several minutes until the butter is well incorporated.

Preheat the oven to 375° F.

Roll out the dough and cut into five equal sections, about 6 inches square, depending on the size of the pears.

Place each pear, wide end down, in the center of a dough square, and draw the dough up around the pears, moistening the four corners slightly and pinching them together gently at the top.

Cut four little collars out of the remaining pastry square, and place one around the stem of each pear, moistening the dough slightly to hold it in place.

Brush each *douillon* with egg yolk.

Place in the preheated oven and cook for 25 to 30 minutes.

Serve the *douillons* with the *crème fraîche* and the vanilla sugar passed separately in bowls.

Note: To make vanilla sugar, bury a vanilla bean in a large glass jar filled with a pound of sugar, close the jar tightly and let stand for a week or two.

Apple Tart
(Tarte aux pommes)

FOR 6 SERVINGS

Pastry:
2 cups flour
Pinch salt
1/2 cup unsalted butter,
slightly softened
1/3 cup water
1 tablespoon sugar
1 egg yolk, beaten

Filling:
7 medium apples
Water
4 to 5 tablespoons sugar
1 egg

Cooking time:
Apples, 15 minutes
Tart, 30 minutes

*I*f you look closely, France is not hexagonal but round, like a tart, and since the Middle Ages tarts have been the recipients of France's abundant and varied local produce. The west of France is the region of apples and pears and, naturally, of apple tarts. The pastry, originally a crude bread dough, has been refined over the centuries, and today can be a delicate *pâtisserie* of considerable finesse.

To make the pastry dough, combine the flour and salt in a mixing bowl. Cut the butter into pieces and cut into the flour, working with a fork until the mixture resembles coarse meal. Add the water a little at a time, tossing it into the mixture with a fork. Add the sugar and roll the dough into a ball. Wrap in a kitchen towel and let rest, refrigerated, for 1/2 hour.

Peel and core the apples. Set three of them aside. Chop the other four coarsely and place in a saucepan with a little water.

Place over medium heat and cook, stirring occasionally and mashing the apples down until they have reduced to a purée. If the apples taste too acidic, stir in a tablespoon of the sugar. Remove from the heat and let cool.

Preheat the oven to 375° F.

On a lightly floured surface, roll out the pastry to an 11-inch round and use it to line the bottom of a buttered 9 to 10-inch tart pan. Prick the bottom and sides of the dough with a fork.

Place in the preheated oven and cook for 15 minutes.

Meanwhile, cut the remaining three apples into very thin slices.

Remove the pie shell from the oven and fill with the apple compote. Arrange the apple slices evenly over the top.

Beat the 4 tablespoons sugar with the egg and spread it over the top of the tart.

Using a brush, coat the edges of the pastry shell with the beaten egg yolk.

Return the pie to the bottom rack of the preheated oven and cook for 15 minutes longer.

Note: Cooking apples work best in this tart—in France, we use *reinettes*. If not available, Ida Red, Cortland, McIntosh or other cooking varieties may be substituted.

Brittany Prune Custard

(Far breton)

*T*his has the consistency of a flan and is cut in large squares or wedges in the pan before serving. Accompany it with a cup of Fouesnant cider, which has a slightly bitter taste and is much appreciated by the local populace. Whether made with prunes (a specialty of Quiberon), or with raisins (as in Brest) or even nature, without any fruit, as in Saint-Pol-de-Leon, fars have just the right touch of sweetness.

Rinse the prunes and place them in a saucepan. Add enough cold water to cover, and cook over low heat for 10 minutes. (They should be tender but still firm.) Drain and remove the pits.

Preheat the oven to 350° F.

Place the milk in a medium saucepan and bring to a boil.

In a large mixing bowl, combine the flour and sugar. Add the eggs one at a time, mixing well after each addition.

Slowly pour the boiling milk over the flour-egg mixture, stirring vigorously with a wooden spoon.

Pour the batter into a buttered baking dish. Place in the preheated oven and cook for 10 minutes.

Remove from the oven and sprinkle the prunes evenly over the top of the batter. Return to the oven to cook about 20 minutes longer, or until the top is nicely browned.

Serve warm or cold.

FOR 6 SERVINGS

1/2 pound prunes
4 cups milk
1 1/2 cups flour
1 cup sugar
4 eggs

Special equipment:
13 by 9 by 2-inch baking dish, preferably earthenware

Cooking time:
30 minutes

In this tour of Alsace, we have annexed the Lorraine and even (forgive us!) Picardie regions. These are all provinces in which no time or effort is spared in day-to-day tasks, where simple home cooking exhibits a touch of genius and where conviviality (a word that is slowly losing its meaning) finds full expression.

Alsace first. It is without a doubt my favorite province after the Lyonnais because of its natural richness, its gentleness and the diversity of its culinary traditions that draw the best from its neighbors. Here is the *savoir-faire* of Eastern territories famous for their *charcuterie*; a profusion of home-made German-style pastries; and the spices and goose dishes of the Jewish communities.

A favorite subject for the Sunday painter, its balconies over-flowing with geraniums, its splendid wine routes lush in autumn, Alsace is a master of culinary sleight of hand. We could swear that a faint scent of soap still hovers around the *baekeofe* (traditionally cooked on wash day), and that there will always be a Hansi (a nineteenth-century Alsatian artist) to capture in pen and ink the arrival of the season's first rhubarb, the dreamy satisfaction of someone sampling a *flammenküche*, and the sparkling eyes of children contemplating holiday tarts.

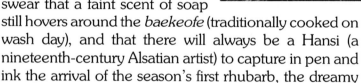

Wild game and freshwater fish are more plentiful and more protected here than anywhere else in France, and, as we know, cabbage has achieved most-favored-vegetable status in Alsace. *Choucroute*, for which there are at least forty methods of preparation, is one of the world's marvels of dining pleasure. The Lorraine, right next door, is a region of springs and streams, chestnut and beech trees, and the soft Meuse hills, all

bathed in the clean air of the Vosges mountains. Famous for its quiche and *potée*, the Lorraine is also known for a remarkable tradition of *charcuterie*, which is clearly implied in the premise that "the only good *boudin* is in Lorraine." When it comes to sweets, this area is right up there with Alsace thanks to its currant jam, whose seeds have been removed with the help of goose quills (Bar-le-Duc), its macaroons (Nancy), its madeleines in chestnut-wood boxes (Commercy) and its *eau-de-vie de mirabelle*, or plum brandy.

Some claim that the difference between the cooking of Lorraine and Alsace is about the same as that between Normandy and Brittany; here too, many dishes feature fresh cream.

And finally, Picardie. Not much is said about this region's culinary accomplishments. I have tried to correct this oversight, linking it (a little arbitrarily, perhaps) to Alsace and Lorraine. If the *flam-iche* tart (with leeks, onion or potatoes) is worth a trip, do not forget that Picardie also produces wonderful meats (particularly those of the Bay of Somme), wild waterfowl in abundance, robust cheeses like the famous Maroilles, and that the duck *pâté* of Amiens is a Picardian specialty that has been renowned in Paris since the seventeenth century.

171

Cherry Soup
(Soupe aux cerises)

*C*herry soup is traditionally served on Christmas night in Alsace. Naturally, the cherries used at this time of year are preserved, part of the wealth of fruits put up during the abundance of summer according to local custom. There is also a sweet-savory version of this soup, and another made with red wine. Mine includes kirsch, an ingredient that, to me, seems indispensable here.

Rinse the cherries and remove their stems. Drain and dry thoroughly.

Place them in a large saucepan with the sugar and kirsch.

Place over medium heat, bring to a boil and let cook for 15 minutes.

Cut the bread into 1/2-inch-thick rounds.

Melt 1 1/2 to 2 tablespoons of the butter in a skillet. When hot, add as many of the bread rounds as will fit comfortably in the skillet and sauté until browned on both sides. Remove and set aside to drain on paper towels. Continue in this manner, adding more butter if necessary, until all the bread rounds are browned. Divide the bread slices among six large shallow serving bowls.

Test a cherry for doneness: it should crush easily between your fingers.

In a small bowl, combine the cornstarch and water.

Using a slotted spoon, remove the cherries from the pan. Add the cornstarch mixture to the pan, stirring vigorously over low heat to thoroughly mix and bind the cherry liquid.

Return the cherries to the pan for a few seconds. Ladle the soup over the toasted bread slices in the soup bowls.

FOR 6 SERVINGS

1 3/4 pounds black cherries
3 tablespoons sugar
2 teaspoons kirsch
1 loaf crusty French-style bread
2 to 3 tablespoons unsalted butter
1 scant tablespoon cornstarch
1 tablespoon cold water

Cooking time:
20 minutes

Ham and Mushroom-Filled Crêpes

(Ficelles picardes)

For the Crêpes:
1 1/2 cups flour
1 1/4 cups milk
2 large eggs
2 tablespoons melted butter
Salt
7 tablespoons beer

For the Filling:
1 pound cultivated mushrooms
Juice of 1 lemon
3 to 4 medium shallots
6 tablespoons unsalted butter
1/4 cup flour
Salt
1 1/2 cups milk
Freshly ground pepper
Oil
6 large thin slices ham
1 1/4 cups *crème fraîche*
1 1/2 cups grated Gruyère cheese

*Cooking time:
About 30 minutes, not including preparation time for crêpes*

Almost all of us have eaten ficelles picardes *at one time or another, often without knowing it. It is a family dish that children love—thin, savory crêpes rolled with a béchamel, mushrooms and ham, and placed in the oven to brown under a layer of cream and grated cheese.*

Since the béchamel sauce and the mushroom duxelle *appeared in French cooking no earlier than the seventeenth century, this favorite could be considered a relatively recent phenomenon.*

To prepare the crêpe batter, place the flour in a mixing bowl. Stir in the cold milk a little at a time to prevent the flour from lumping. Add the eggs and melted butter, season lightly with salt and beat well. Set aside in a cool place for at least 1 1/2 hours. (The beer is added just before cooking the crêpes.)

Trim and rinse the mushrooms, wipe dry. Chop the mushrooms, place them in a bowl with the lemon juice and toss. Peel and finely chop the shallots.

Melt 2 tablespoons of the butter, add the shallots and cook until wilted. Add mushrooms and cook for 10 minutes.

To make the béchamel, melt 4 tablespoons of the butter in a saucepan, stir in the flour and a little salt and cook, stirring, until mixture froths, without letting it color. Remove from the heat, and stir in the milk, whisking vigorously. Return to the heat and cook, stirring, until the sauces boils and thickens. Stir the mushroom and shallot mixture into the sauce. Season lightly with pepper and more salt, if necessary.

Whisk the beer into the crêpe batter. Oil an 8 1/2-inch non-stick crêpe pan and place over medium-high heat until hot. Add a few tablespoons of the batter, swirling the pan quickly to distribute evenly, and cook until lightly browned on both sides. Continue until all the batter is used. (You should have about 12 crêpes.)

Preheat the oven to 400° F.

Cut the ham slices in half and lay a piece on each crêpe. Spread the béchamel sauce over the ham, and roll each crêpe up as tightly as possible to form a *ficelle* (string). Place the crêpes side by side in a buttered baking dish. Spoon the *crème fraîche* over them and sprinkle with the grated cheese.

Let heat and brown in the preheated oven for 10 minutes. Serve immediately.

Savory Bacon and Onion Tart

(Tarte à la flamme)

*T*he name literally translates into "flame-cooked tart," as this pie was traditionally cooked in the baker's wood-fired oven. Today it shows up at all the region's wine festivals and fairs, and it is eaten piping hot right out of the open-air ovens in which it cooks.

If using frozen bread dough, thaw according to package directions.

Cut the bacon into 1/4 by 1/4 by 1-inch pieces, removing any rind. Blanch it in a saucepan of boiling water for 1 minute, rinse under cold water, drain and pat dry. Peel and chop the onions.

Melt the butter in a large skillet, add the onions and sauté until wilted but not browned.

Combine the *fromage blanc* and the *crème fraîche* in a bowl. Season lightly with salt and stir in 4 tablespoons of the oil.

Preheat the oven to 475° F.

On a lightly floured surface, roll out the bread dough as thinly as possible into a rectangle. Place it on a lightly buttered baking sheet. Turn up the edges and roll them to form a rim around the tart.

Spread the sautéed onions evenly over the bottom of the pastry shell. Sprinkle the bacon over the onions. Spoon the cheese and cream mixture over the top. Drizzle the remaining 2 tablespoons oil over all.

Place in the oven and cook for about 10 minutes. Serve immediately.

FOR 6 SERVINGS

1 pound bread dough
1/2 pound slab bacon
2 medium onions
2 tablespoons unsalted butter
5 1/3 ounces *fromage blanc* or 1/2 cup whipped cream cheese
3/4 cups *crème fraîche* or heavy cream
Salt
6 tablespoons vegetable oil

Cooking time:
About 15 minutes

174

Leek and Cream Tourte

(Flamiche)

Pastry:
1 1/2 cups flour
Pinch salt
3/4 cup unsalted butter
1/4 cup (2 ounces) lard,
suet or solid shortening
1 tablespoon baking
powder
1 egg yolk
1/3 cup water

Filling:
15 large leeks
Coarse salt
3 tablespoons unsalted
butter
1/4 cup flour
1 cup *crème fraîche*
or heavy cream
Fine salt
Freshly ground pepper
Grated nutmeg
1 egg yolk

Cooking time:
Filling, 30 minutes
Tourte, 30 minutes

*A*lso called flamique, *this is to the Picardie region what quiche is to Lorraine. Whether it takes the form of a tart or a covered* tourte, *the most common version is made with leeks. It is eaten as a first course, accompanied by a glass of good local beer.*

To make the pastry, place the flour and salt in a large mixing bowl. Cut the butter and lard into small pieces, add to the flour, and work the ingredients together with the fingertips. Add the baking powder, egg yolk, and just enough water to make a smooth, soft dough. Roll into a ball and let rest while preparing the filling.

Trim the leeks of all but the white parts, wash thoroughly, and drain. Drop them a few at a time into a large saucepan of boiling water seasoned with coarse salt and blanch for 2 minutes. Drain the leeks and rinse under cold water.

Return the leeks to the boiling salted water and cook for 10 minutes.

Drain the leeks, reserving about 3/4 cup of the liquid in which they cooked. Dry on paper towels.

Melt the butter in a saucepan. Stir in the flour and cook briefly without allowing the mixture to brown. Add 1/2 cup of the reserved leek broth, stirring with a wooden spoon. Stir in the cream and cook, stirring, over medium-low heat for 7 to 10 minutes. Season with salt, pepper, and nutmeg.

Cut the leeks into 1-inch pieces and add to the sauce.

Preheat the oven to 400° F.

Divide the pastry dough into two parts: two-thirds and one-third. Roll the larger portion out into an 11-inch round and use it to line a buttered 9 to 10-inch *tourte* pan or deep-sided cake pan, allowing the pastry to spill over the rim.

Prick the bottom of the pastry with a fork. Pour the leek mixture into the *tourte.*

Roll out the remaining pastry into a 9 to 10-inch round and place it over the top of the *tourte.* Moisten the edges of both pastry rounds with a little water and press them firmly together with the fingertips. Trim off excess dough.

Insert a short length of rolled cardboard into the center of the pastry to form a pipe for steam to escape.

Beat the egg yolk and brush it over the top and rim of the pastry. Place in the preheated oven and cook for 30 minutes.

Cheese and Bacon Custard Tart

(Quiche lorraine)

Culinary texts show that quiche lorraine appeared around the end of the sixteenth century, well before Stanislas Leczynski, former king of Poland, made the city of Nancy a capital of good living and dining. A variation of the German *kuchen (cake),* the quiche of today is served throughout France, filled with the best of local products. Since the Lorraine region is noted for its charcuterie and pork products, it is only natural that a dice of delicate smoked bacon should be mixed with the cream and eggs in this dish.

Preheat the oven to 450° F.

Line a buttered 9 to 10-inch tart mold with the pastry.

Dice the bacon and ham into small cubes, removing any rind.

Melt the butter in a skillet, add the bacon and sauté until lightly browned. Drain and spread over the bottom of the tart shell. Sprinkle the cubed ham evenly over the shell.

Break two of the eggs into a mixing bowl. Separate the whites from the yolks of the remaining two eggs, adding the yolks to the mixing bowl with the whole eggs. (Reserve the whites for another use.)

Beat the eggs and yolks with a fork, incorporating the cream. Season with the salt, pepper, nutmeg and chives. Stir in the cheese.

Turn the mixture into the tart shell. Place in the preheated oven and cook for about 30 minutes.

FOR 6 SERVINGS

1 round prepared pastry (1/2 of a 15-ounce package)
1/2 pound smoked slab bacon
1 thick slice boiled ham (3 1/2 ounces)
1 1/2 tablespoons unsalted butter
4 eggs
1 1/4 cup light cream
Salt
Freshly ground pepper
Freshly grated nutmeg
1 teaspoon chopped chives
1 cup (3 1/2 ounces) diced Gruyère or Swiss cheese

Cooking time:
About 35 minutes.

178

Alsatian Wash-Day Stew

(Baekeofe)

This dish can also be called potée boulangère (baker's wife's stew). Not so long ago, it was common for cooks in France to bring oven-ready dishes, from chicken stew to tarts, to the corner baker to be cooked in his roomy wood-fired oven.

In Alsace, the big earthenware casserole presented to the baker for slow simmering often contained pork and sliced potatoes in alternating layers, and sometimes mutton or beef. Local tradition elected Monday baekeofe day, since it was wash day and there was little time to tend to dinner. Assembled a day in advance, the baekeofe required nothing more than a trip to the bakery, where it would simmer away next to other stews in one of two hot brick ovens.

The success of this dish depends partly on the vessel in which it cooks. The best is a large earthenware, ovenproof casserole with a tight-fitting lid to keep the stew tender and hold in all its flavor.

A day in advance, cut the lamb, beef and pork into thick slices and place them in a large bowl. Add the wine.

Trim and thoroughly wash the leeks. Cut into short lengths. Peel and chop 2 of the onions. Peel the garlic cloves.

Add the leeks, onions, garlic cloves (whole), and bouquet garni to the bowl with the meat. Season with salt and pepper. Cover and let marinate overnight, refrigerated, stirring two or three times to allow the marinade to soak into the meat.

The following day, peel the remaining onions and the potatoes.

Slice the potatoes into rounds. Chop the onions.

Using a slotted spoon, remove the meat from the marinade. Drain the marinade through a fine sieve.

Cut the pigs' feet in half lengthwise. Blanch them in a large pan of boiling water for 5 minutes. Drain thoroughly.

Preheat the oven to 350° F.

Place a layer of potatoes in the bottom of a large, deep, ovenproof baking dish (preferably earthenware). Sprinkle with some of the chopped onions. Add a layer of meat, followed by two halves of the split pigs' feet. Continue to layer the ingredients in this manner, alternating potatoes, onions, and meat, seasoning between layers with salt and pepper.

FOR 10 SERVINGS

1 3/4 pounds boned shoulder of lamb
1 3/4 pounds boned shoulder of beef
1 3/4 pounds shoulder of pork
4 cups white wine, preferably Riesling or Sylvaner
5 leeks
5 medium onions
8 cloves garlic
1 bouquet garni
Salt
Freshly ground pepper
6 1/2 pounds potatoes
2 pigs' feet
Water
Flour

Cooking time:
3 1/4 hours

180

Dilute the marinade with about 4 cups water, and add to the baking dish.

In a small bowl, combine enough flour and water to make a sticky dough. Form it into a long cord and place it around the rim of the baking dish. Moisten the edge of the dish cover with warm water and press down firmly on the dough to form a seal.

Place the baking dish over medium heat just long enough to start the cooking. Then transfer to the preheated oven and let cook for 3 hours.

When cooked, remove the large slices of meat and cut them into pieces to allow everyone to taste some of each. Serve with a simple salad.

Alsatian-style Sauerkraut

(Choucroute garnie à l'alsacienne)

A"Frenchification" of the German word sauerkraut (literally, bitter grass), choucroute is, first of all, fermented cabbage, and secondly, the main ingredient in the hearty one-dish meal to which it lends its name. This typically Alsatian preparation, now considered a national specialty, has been around for centuries. It evidently existed in the 1500s, accompanied by strange garnishments, including fried herring, salmon, and snails. For those who believe that choucroute au poisson is an invention of nouvelle cuisine, this is sure proof to the contrary. Nevertheless, choucroute garnie more commonly features pork. In this recipe, I have used pork knuckle, shoulder and bacon, as well as several kinds of sausages. In fact, this is what some Parisian restaurants would call a choucroute royale.

Place the pork knuckle, shoulder, slab bacon, and pickled breast in a large saucepan or stock pot. Cover them with cold water, bring to a simmer, and let simmer gently for about 30 minutes, skimming off from time to time the foam that rises to the surface.

Rinse the sauerkraut in several changes of cold water. Drain thoroughly, squeezing balls of it firmly between the palms of the hands to extract as much water as possible.

Peel and chop the onions. Peel and mash the garlic cloves. Tie the juniper berries, peppercorns, thyme, and bay leaf together in a small square of cheesecloth.

Preheat the oven to 350° F.

Heat all but 2 tablespoons of the goose fat in a large cast-iron Dutch oven. Add the onions and sauté until wilted. Add the sauerkraut and stir well to coat thoroughly with the fat.

Add the garlic and the spice pouch. Pour in the wine and bouillon (or water), stir and cover. Place in the preheated oven to cook for 45 minutes.

Remove the pan from the oven and remove half of the sauerkraut (it should still be slightly crunchy). Remove the pork knuckle, shoulder, bacon, and breast from the pan in which they simmered and drain. (Reserve this liquid for poaching the frankfurters.) Arrange them over the sauerkraut in the Dutch oven.

Cover with the remaining sauerkraut. Return to the oven and cook 30 to 40 minutes longer.

FOR 6 SERVINGS

1 large pickled pork knuckle
1 smoked pork shoulder
2/3 pound smoked slab bacon
2/3 pound pickled pork breast (see note)
3 1/2 pounds raw sauerkraut
2 onions
2 cloves garlic
15 juniper berries
6 peppercorns
1 sprig thyme
1/2 bay leaf
3 1/2 ounces rendered goose fat (about 7 tablespoons) or duck fat, or a mixture of rendered bacon fat and oil
2 cups dry white wine, preferably Sylvaner
1 1/2 cups bouillon or water
4 smoked Montbéliard sausages (see note)
6 good quality frankfurters
6 small blood sausages
1/2 pound veal sausages
Salt

Cooking time:
About 2 1/2 hours

Add the Montbéliard sausages and let cook for 40 minutes longer.

Just before serving, melt the remaining goose fat in a skillet. Add the blood and veal sausages and sauté until lightly browned.

Add the frankfurters to the pan in which the pork meats simmered and poach gently.

Remove the pan from the oven, and arrange the sauerkraut and meats on a large earthenware platter, discarding the spice pouch. Arrange the sausages over the top and serve, accompanied by boiled potatoes.

Note: If you can not find pickled pork breast, blanch a raw pork breast in boiling salted water and drain. Then simmer it in a saucepan of water with a bay leaf for about 1 hour before proceeding with the recipe.

Montbéliard are small smoked sausages weighing 3 to 4 ounces each. Other smoked pork sausages such as small, good quality kabanos or kielbasa can be substituted. Bratwurst and other German-style sausages can be substituted for the blood and veal sausages, if preferred.

184

Chestnut Purée and Cream

(Mont-blanc)

This is a cold dessert that is very easy to prepare. A family specialty for children with a sweet tooth, it is also included in the repertoire of classic pastry-making. For those who really love chestnuts, shavings of marrons glacés *(rich candied chestnuts) can be sprinkled over the top.*

FOR 8 SERVINGS

3 1/3 pounds fresh chestnuts
4 cups milk
1 vanilla bean
1 cup granulated sugar
7 tablespoons butter
1 cup whipping cream
1 teaspoon powdered sugar
2 tablespoons vanilla sugar (see note), or 2 tablespoons sugar and a few drops vanilla extract

Cooking time:
Chestnuts, 45 minutes

Cut a cross in the rounded side of each chestnut shell with the point of a small knife. Place the chestnuts in a large saucepan, add enough cold water to cover, and bring to a boil over medium-high heat. Boil for 1 minute. Drain. When cool enough to handle, peel them, removing the outer shell, as well as the inner membrane.

Place the milk in a saucepan with the vanilla bean, broken in half lengthwise, and bring to a boil over medium heat. Stir in the granulated sugar and the peeled chestnuts, and let cook over very low heat for 45 minutes. Meanwhile, remove the butter from the refrigerator, chop coarsely and let soften slightly.

Drain the chestnuts. Place them in a food mill fitted with a large-hole disk, and press them out slowly, adding the butter a little at a time. Spoon this chestnut "vermicelli" into a charlotte or ring mold, without mashing them down. Place in the refrigerator and chill for 30 minutes.

Just before serving, combine the cream, powdered sugar and vanilla sugar in a bowl and whip.

Turn the chestnut mixture out of the mold onto a serving platter.

Decorate with the whipped cream squeezed through a pastry bag, preferably fitted with a serrated tip.

Note: To make vanilla sugar, bury a vanilla bean in a large glass jar filled with a pound of sugar, close the jar tightly and let sit for a week or two.

Alsatian
Tart with
Fresh
Cheese

(Tarte
alsacienne au
fromage blanc)

FOR 8 SERVINGS

14 ounces puff pastry
2 cups milk
1 pound *fromage blanc*
(see note)
1 1/3 cups sugar
1 cup flour
3 eggs
3/4 cup *crème fraîche*
or heavy cream

*Cooking time:
About 40 minutes*

Here is a tart that appears on holidays next to all the fruit tarts that make Alsace a region of a thousand colors. This fresh cheese tart, sometimes called mangin *when it includes cream, can be eaten warm or cold.*

Preheat the oven to 400° F.

On a lightly floured surface, roll out the puff pastry to a 15-inch round and use it to line a buttered 12 to 13-inch tart mold (preferably with removable bottom). Prick the bottom of the pastry with a fork.

Place the milk in a small saucepan and warm over low heat.

Place the *fromage blanc* into a fine sieve and drain off excess liquid. Turn the drained cheese into a large mixing bowl.

Stir in the sugar. Add the flour. Stir in the eggs one at a time. Stir in the cream.

Stirring constantly, add the warm milk a little at a time to the mixing bowl.

Turn the batter into the pie shell.

Place in the preheated oven and cook for 35 minutes.

When the pie is done, turn off the oven and let the pie cook in the residual heat for 5 to 6 minutes with the oven door open. Unmold immediately onto a cake rack and allow to cool slightly.

Serve warm or cold.

Note: If *fromage blanc* is not available, use 1 pound well-drained California-style (small curd) cottage cheese. To drain, line a sieve with a double layer of cheesecloth. Turn the cottage cheese into the sieve, and gather up the corners of the cheesecloth to meet in the middle. Gently squeeze out excess liquid. Process the drained cottage cheese in a food processor until smooth.

Rhubarb Tart

(Tarte à la rhubarbe)

In Alsace, the first rhubarb of spring goes into a pie. There is plenty of time before July to make compotes and jams with the rest of the harvest.

Until the eighteenth century, rhubarb, like asparagus, was classed as a medicinal plant, or was used only for decoration. The English were the first take the plunge and try it in a pie.

In a large mixing bowl, combine the flour, baking powder, and salt. Make a well in the center and add the oil, a tablespoon at a time, stirring vigorously after each addition to incorporate it into the flour.

Slowly stir in the water. Add the egg and beat well. The dough should be relatively moist.

Do not let the dough rest, but turn it into a buttered 10-inch tart pan, and using the fingertips or the back of a spoon, spread it out evenly over the bottom and sides of the pan.

Preheat the oven to 400° F.

Trim and peel the rhubarb, stripping away the large fibers. Cut the ribs into 1 1/2-inch lengths and spread them evenly over the tart shell.

In a mixing bowl, combine the egg and sugar and beat until the mixture turns a light lemon yellow.

Turn the egg and sugar mixture into the tart shell, spreading it out evenly.

Place in the preheated oven and cook for about 35 minutes.

Serve warm or cold.

FOR 4 SERVINGS

Pastry:
1 1/4 cups flour
1 tablespoon baking powder
1/8 teaspoon salt
1/2 cup oil
2 tablespoons water
1 egg

Filling:
4 large ribs rhubarb
1 egg
6 tablespoons sugar

*Cooking time:
35 minutes*

188

Damson Plum Tart

(Tarte aux quetsches)

FOR 8 SERVINGS

Pastry:
2/3 cup unsalted butter, softened
2 eggs
1 egg yolk
2 1/2 cups flour
1/2 cup granulated sugar
Pinch salt

Filling:
2 1/2-3 pounds Damson plums
1 tablespoon flour
1 tablespoon granulated sugar
1/4 cup powdered sugar

*Cooking time:
30 minutes*

It is said in Alsace that the famous apple offered by Eve and swallowed by Adam, was actually a plum. Everyone here has his own local source for this fruit. Plum tart, slightly acidic, is in season whenever there is a holiday, and takes its place next to tarts filled with cherry plums, apples, fromage blanc and jam.

There is no skimping on desserts in Alsace, and, though it is nearly possible to name the seasons by the fillings in the tarts, plums have been available year-round since the fifteenth century, when people first began drying them in bread ovens.

Prepare the pastry dough 2 hours in advance: Place the softened butter in a mixing bowl. Add the eggs and egg yolk, one at a time, stirring with a wooden spoon until thoroughly incorporated into the butter.

Place the flour in a large mixing bowl and make a well in the center. Add the egg-butter mixture, using your fingertips to gradually incorporate the flour. Add the sugar and salt and blend well. Roll the dough into a ball and let rest in the refrigerator for 2 hours.

Rinse and carefully dry the plums. Using a sharp knife, split them open and remove the pits.

Preheat the oven to 475° F.

When the dough has rested, turn it out onto a lightly floured surface and roll it out with a rolling pin, then continue to work it by stretching it out by hand. Use it to line a buttered 9 to 10-inch tart pan. Prick the bottom and sides of the pastry with a fork.

In a small bowl, combine the flour and sugar. Sprinkle it evenly over the tart shell to prevent the pastry from softening.

Arrange the plums in the tart shell, placing them upright and packing them as closely together as possible. Sprinkle with the powdered sugar.

Place in the preheated oven and cook for 30 minutes.

189

Index

190

Photographic acknowledgements

The photographs are by Dietmar Frege, except for the following:

p. 1–2–3–4–5: J.-P. Dieterlen; p. 10–11: Scope/ J.-L. Barde; p. 12: Scope/ J.-L. Barde (top), Scope/ J. Sierpinski (bottom); p. 13: Scope/ J.-L. Barde (top), Diaf/ P. Somelet (top); p. 33: Diaf/ P. Somelet; p. 62: Scope/ J.-D. Sudres; p. 64–65: Scope/ J.-D. Sudres; p. 66: Scope/ D. Faure (top); p. 67: Scope/ J. Sierpinski; p. 72: Top/ P. Hussenot; p. 73: Diaf/ L. Devémy (top); p. 77: Top/ P. Hussenot; p. 95: Rapho/ Pasquier; p. 95: Scope/ J. Guillard; p. 98–99: Scope/ M. Guillard; p.100: Scope/ M. Guillard; p. 101: Scope/ J.-D. Sudres (top), Scope/ M. Guillard (bottom and center);

p. 118–119: Scope/ J.-D. Sudres; p. 120: Scope/ J.-D. Sudres; p. 121: Scope/ M. Guillard; p. 125: Scope/ J.-D. Sudres; p. 129: Scope/ J.-L. Barde; p. 130: Scope/ J.-D. Sudres; p. 132–133: Scope/ J. Guillard; p. 134: Scope/ J.-D. Sudres (top), Scope/ J. Guillard (bottom); p. 135: Scope/ J. Guillard (top); p. 144: Top/ Gazuit; p. 159: Top/ R. Mazin; p. 164: Diaf/ D. Souse; p. 165: Scope/ J. Guillard; p. 168–169: Top/ P. Hussenot; p. 170: Scope/ J.-D. Sudres (top); p. 171: Scope/ J.-L. Barde (top), Scope/J. Guillard (bottom); p. 172: Scope/ J.-D. Sudres; p. 176: Top/ R. Mazin; p. 181: Scope/ J. Guillard; p. 184: Top/ L. Rousseau; p. 185: Scope/ M. Guillard; p. 186: Scope/ J.-D. Sudres; p. 189: Scope/ J.-L. Barde.

Library of Congress Cataloging-in-Publication Data

Bocuse, Paul, 1926–
    [Cuisine de France. English]
    Paul Bocuse's regional French cooking / with the assistance of Martine Albertin, Anne Grandclément, and Pascale Couderc ; translated by Stephanie Curtis ; recipes adapted from the French by Stephanie Curtis and Charles Pierce ; photography by Dietmar Frege. — 1st paperback ed.
        p.   cm.
    Includes index.
    ISBN 2-08-013641-0
    1. Cookery, French. I. Albertin, Martine. II. Grandclément, Anne. III. Coudrec, Pascale. IV. Title.
[TX719.B671713 1997]
641.5944—dc21
                                         96–51640